girlfriends

Other books by
Carmen Renee Berry and Tamara Traeder

The girlfriends Keepsake Book:
The Story of Our Friendship
(Wildcat Canyon Press, 1996)

girlfriends Talk About Men:
Sharing Secrets for a Great Relationship
(Wildcat Canyon Press, 1997)

girlfriends

Invisible Bonds, Enduring Ties

CARMEN RENEE BERRY AND TAMARA TRAEDER

WILDCAT CANYON PRESS
A Division of Circulus Publishing Group, Inc.
Berkeley, California

Senior Editor: Roy M. Carlisle
Copyeditor: Priscilla Stuckey
Cover and Interior Design: Gordon Chun Design
Printed in the United States of America

Library of Congress Cataloging-in-Publication Data

Berry, Carmen Renee.
    Girlfriends: invisible bonds, enduring ties / Carmen Renee Berry
and Tamara Traeder. — 1st ed.
      p.   cm.
ISBN 1-885171-08-0 (pbk.)
      1. Women—Psychology. 2. Friendship. 3. Interpersonal relations.
I. Traeder, Tamara, 1960–   . II. Title.
HQ1206.B38 1995
305.4—dc20   95-36542   CIP

Distributed to the trade by Publishers Group West
35 34 33 32 31 30 29 28 27

Contents

*To all of our beloved girlfriends who were woefully
neglected while we were hiding away writing about the joys
and triumphs of friendships. Thanks for hanging in there
and we'll be in touch soon!*

Acknowledgments

We are grateful to the women of all ages, backgrounds, and races who so graciously and candidly shared their stories with us. Without you, this book would have never been produced.

For believing in us and this project, we thank our parents, Gus Traeder and Fern Traeder, Dr. David A. Berry and Mary Ellen Berry, as well as our friends Wynn McClenahan, Nancy Dusseau, Nancy Ryan, Betsy Brady, Mark Baker, Rene Chansler, Gail Walker, Pat Luehrs, Lynn Barrington, Cathy Smith, Bob Parsons, Joel Miller, Connie Lillas, Trevor Dobbs, Irene Fores, Cynthia Bell, Bobette Buster, Bob Myers, John Kitzmiller, and Leon Bass, Jr.

Tamara gives special thanks to Laura Rafaty, who read the manuscript in its various stages and provided many valuable suggestions, and Linda Williams, for proofreading the manuscript and sharing her worthy insights. She also is most grateful to Peter Graves, who has provided gracious support and steady enthusiasm through the vicissitudes of this project.

Carmen extends special thanks to her colleagues at Christian Recovery International who provided superhuman support during an especially stressful time, including Dale Ryan, Dale and Sara Wolery, Virginia and John

Frederich, Paula Neal Reza, Susan Latta, David and Wendy Wilkinson and Lori Wolery. She also appreciates the nurturing hands of her body work and massage therapists for helping her deal with the stress, Mandy Stephen, Claudette Renner, and Carolyn Braddock. Last, but not least, Carmen is grateful to her therapist, Dr. Paul Roberts and the support of Victor Parra through this significant period of time.

We give a standing ovation to Julie Bennett for conceiving the initial vision for this book, and for giving us both the opportunity to birth it together. Special thanks goes to Roy M. Carlisle for his unique editorial contribution and emotional support throughout the process. We thank Priscilla Stuckey for insightful copyediting, and Gordon Chun Design for the intuitive design. We also are most grateful to Holly A. Taines for her help in revising this manuscript and tracking down sources and crucial pieces of paper which kept drifting out of control and to Molly Bennett for sacrificing part of her summer vacation for this project. Thank you all.

Telling Our Stories

From the kitchen she hears laughter,
and the clatter of dishes.
Charis is setting out the food,
Roz is telling a story.
That's what they will do,
increasingly in their lives:
tell stories.

—MARGARET ATWOOD
The Robber Bride

I feel there is something unexplored about women that only a woman can explore.

—GEORGIA O'KEEFE

"She is always there for me." "I can tell her anything." "I don't know what I would do without her." These are some common responses we received when we asked women to comment on their women friends. Girlfriends are those women who know us better than anyone (sometimes better than we know ourselves). They are not only essential for coping with our day-to-day frustrations or sharing private jokes, they help us limp through a crisis and, in the long run, help us grow as women and human beings. Our girlfriends say much about who we are—where we are in our lives, what aspects of ourselves we value or are trying to develop. These are invaluable relationships, and we would like to explore them.

Why are these relationships so important to us? One reason that friendships are so important to women may lie in the very fact that we are women. Researchers in recent years have begun to provide support for the notion that women's development is different than that of men, and that as women we develop as persons by our connections with others, as opposed to the development of men, in which "high value is placed on autonomy, self-reliance, independence, self-actualization, 'listening to and following' one's own unique dream, destiny and fulfillment."[1] Psychologist Jean Baker Miller wrote, "Women's sense of self becomes very much organized around being able to make and then to maintain affiliation and relationships."[2] Relationships, therefore, are a crucial component of our development.

Relationships with women are especially important because we need other women as models, models whose circumstances are close to our own. As mirrors of our experience, our girlfriends provide an empathetic guide for our behavior. We look to women and their experiences in order to start defining ourselves as women, to value ourselves as human beings.

Historically, women all over the world have been defined and valued by their relationships with men — legally, morally and socially. Even in the United States, a relatively young country, the American woman began her journey under the official declaration that "all *men* are created equal" (emphasis added). Abigail Adams tried to influence her husband and co-composer of the Declaration of Independence, John Adams, to "remember the ladies, and be more generous and favorable to them than your ancestors. Do not put such unlimited power into the hands of the Husbands."[3] John Adams responded with "We know better than to repeal our Masculine systems."[4] Unable to own property or retain custody of their own children, women were left with wondering about who they were, where they fit in and how they fared in relation to

4

others. These women were defined legally by their relationships to men — as wives, mothers, sisters, or daughters.

Not only was a woman's legal role defined by her relationship with men, but her moral classification as a woman was determined from her behavior with men. The "good" woman was one who resembled the Virgin Mary, the pure, spiritual wife who, apparently without sex (or at least without enjoying it) becomes the nurturing, selfless mother. However, in the event that a wife no longer served her husband to his liking, she would become "bad," referred to as the "old ball and chain" or the "old lady" and described as nagging, frigid, and overly emotional.

On the other end of town, women of ill repute were also named according to their behavior with men. A woman defined as a prostitute or whore was inherently "bad" and received judgments of promiscuity, being unladylike, and "asking for it." That is, of course, unless men chose to declare such behavior as "sensuous, exciting, playful and responsive," which made the prostitute "good."[5]

A woman's social status was also determined by the status of her husband and father. It was a shame to be born to a father who was poor or "low class," and this could only be remedied by the woman "snagging" a man who could elevate her social status. Marrying the local doctor or lawyer was the dream (or the expected goal) of every young maiden, and upon closing the deal (getting married), she was automatically lifted to a higher social plane. Conversely, women who married "below their station" were considered foolish and forever banished to a lower social status. Those who were the most unfortunate—completely disconnected to men by marriage—were sadly and disparagingly referred to as "old maids" or "spinsters."

This scenario was not satisfactory for many women, and Abigail Adams' warning to her husband seemed to come to fruition. She wrote, "If particular care and attention is not paid to the ladies, we are determined to foment a rebellion, and will not hold ourselves bound by any laws in which we have no voice, or representation."[6] Her warning proved prophetic as women learned to read, demanded the right to vote, and insisted that we too were equal. But equal to what and whom? Equal to men? Does that mean we are like them?

YOU'VE COME A LONG WAY?

Over the last two centuries, through legal changes, power shifts and the invention of television, two popular options for women have emerged: either stick with the program and define ourselves by our relationships with men, or redefine ourselves by becoming like men. Jacqueline Kennedy Onassis put it succinctly, "There are two kinds of women: those who want power in the world, and those who want power in bed."[7] What's a woman to choose? To be "dependent, passive, nurturing types, uninterested in competition, achievement, or success, who should conform to the wishes of the men in their lives,"[8] or to define ourselves primarily by our careers and insist on financial independence?

Many women have recognized that either option represents a dead end for women, for in both cases, women are still defined by a standard derived from men. And the choices we are left with remain hopelessly contradictory. Susan Douglas writes, in her witty and insightful assessment, *Where the Girls Are:*

> Historians will argue, and rightly so, that American women have been surrounded by contradictory expectations since at least the nineteenth century.[9] . . . American women today are a bundle of contradictions because much of the media imagery we grew up with was itself filled with mixed messages about what women should and should not do. . . . The media, of course, urged us to be pliant, cute, sexually available, thin, blond, poreless, wrinkle-free, and deferential to men. But it is easy to forget that the media also suggested that we could be rebellious, tough, enterprising, and shrewd.[10]

Both of these identities are rooted in our relationships with men, either as service providers or as competitors. When we look to men as reference points, however, we lose sight of who we are as women. It is like trying to define an apple by comparing it to an orange. The apple, described in terms of the orange, will never have its own identity, appeal, and value; it will simply be "not an orange." Similarly, defining women in the context of men means that we are defined as "not men" and, unfortunately, frequently viewed as inferior. We as women regain our worth by defining or naming ourselves as women instead of "not men."

We believe we redefine our womanhood within the context of our relationships with women—with our girlfriends. And how do we do that? By telling our stories as women, from the perspective of women. The act of putting our experiences into words and presenting full, true descriptions of our worlds helps to make us three-dimensional beings; we describe ourselves as apples instead of "not oranges." We agree with psychiatrist Olga Knopf when she asserts, "The art of being a woman can never consist of being a bad imitation of a man."[11] Being a woman means finding the source of our power and identity, not in the bedroom or the board room, but in living each day out of the richness of our feminine creativity and passion. We express ourselves as women by drawing from our femininity, not from our nonmaleness.

As we stumble, bumble, and define ourselves into the next century, we women need each other more than ever before—to share our experiences, to struggle for understanding, to create new meaning, to enjoy each other, and to figure out what in the world we are doing with ourselves. Because our female friends share with us the experience of being women, our feminine paths and identities are clarified for us. Author Sue Monk Kidd expressed it this way in an interview: "One thing I realized about having a girlfriend is that I can't tell you who I am without telling you who my girlfriend is. Our relationships with other women are part of the ground of our being. So I can't say who I am without talking about my female friend and who she is in my life. We discover ourselves through our girl-friends; it's a mutual process of self-discovery that goes on when we enter into this kind of female relationship. It's really a process, not just discovering the other person, but of discovering yourself."

A FRIEND IS A FRIEND. WHO CARES ABOUT GENDER?

But really now, what is so special about female friends? Why distinguish female from male friends, can't men give what women can give in a relationship? Not according to many women we interviewed for this book.

These women said that their bonds to men were quite strong but nevertheless different from their relationships with women. Some women find their women friends more intuitive than their male friends. Carey, an attorney in her midthirties, told us, "My husband is my best friend. I have a great relationship with him, and I do not know what I would do without him. Nonetheless, he does not replace my girlfriends; I need them just as much as I always did. It is hard to explain how my relationship with my husband differs from my girlfriends. He lacks a certain intuitive sense that most of my female friends have, but he knows me very well and can provide insights no one else does."

Other women find that conversations with male friends tend to focus more on ideas or problem solving, with less focus on the sharing of feelings. For example, Rachel Anne, a retired professor in her seventies, told us, "I have a few friendships with men. They are more intellectual, academic, and professional than my relationships with women." This sentiment was echoed by Sonja, a human resources director in her early forties: "My relationships with men are quite different from those with women. We concentrate more on philosophizing, not so much on feelings or the other sex." Carolyn told us, "Men are different from my girlfriends precisely because they are men! They communicate differently, much more a combination of banter and serious political/philosophical discussion." And we had to laugh when Julie, managing director of an opera company in her midthirties, put it succinctly, "Men just aren't like women. They see things and solve problems in different ways. They don't like to talk about their feelings, and women thrive on it."

But what is so special about women talking with *women*? Wouldn't a sensitive man do just as well? Many women say that their women friends respond to their problems differently than do most of the men in their lives. While men tend toward a fix-it approach, women often simply provide a listening, sympathetic ear. As Deborah Tannen explains in *You Just Don't Understand: Women and Men in Conversation*, women are often looking "for an expression of understanding ('I know how you feel') or a similar complaint ('I felt the same way when something similar happened to me'). . . . Women are frustrated when they not only don't get this reinforcement but, quite the opposite, feel distanced by the advice which seems to send the ... [message], 'We're not the same. You have the problems; I have the solutions.'"[12]

In addition, men characteristically withhold personal information. In fact, one study conducted by Jack Sattel illustrated that men gain power over women by giving minimal personal information, while encouraging women to self-disclose. Women may often feel uncomfortable, even if consciously unaware, of this power imbalance and find less satisfaction in conversations with men.[13]

Another distinction pointed out by the women we interviewed was to simply state the obvious. Men are not women and so relating to men is, by definition, a different experience. Whether the cause is genetic or environmental, men and women experience life differently. One group has experienced centuries of overt power, while the other is just trying to get the hang of it; one group frets about the size of their penises and the other about the size of their breasts, one group is rewarded for sexual conquests while the other worries about pregnancy; one group shaves their faces and the other shaves their legs. No matter how sensitive a man may be, he is not a woman and, by definition, he lives life from a different perspective than that of a woman.

Helen, a retired real estate agent in her sixties, who we interviewed, concurred by saying that "men don't feel the same passion for the things women deem important. Men seem to think in black and white realities while women feel in vivid colors where nothing is cut and dried. I *need* to talk of 'womanly things' with other women! I tend to keep men friends for the things of the world, the tangible, the 'practical.' Women are concerned about those things and our views add depth to the nuts and bolts of the day-to-day stuff."

Only another woman knows what it is like to be a woman. Only another woman will laugh with you until you both cry, remembering the first time you used a tampon, aided by your best girlfriend who stood outside the bathroom stall shouting insertion instructions. Only another woman can appreciate the bowl which you found for the end table in your living room which has all the colors in your room, and which you bargained with the seller at an antiques fair down to $4.50. Only another woman can understand all the terrible feelings shivering through you when you tell her, "I found a lump in my breast."

Aside from the contrast in male and female experiences, another difference between women's friendships with men and their friendships with women raised by the women we interviewed relates to the "sex" deal. Lesbians, however, may have to resolve sexual tensions with female friends as well as men who may be attracted to them. Most women we interviewed echoed Janet's statement that her "male friendships are usually based on sexual interest by at least one party." While some women observed that their relationships with men were the same as with women, others agreed with Harry in the movie *When Harry Met Sally,* that friendship between men and women is impossible because of the sexual attraction. Harry insisted that sex was the only genuine reason any man was in a so-called "friendship" and once that desire was fulfilled (or all hope was lost for consummation) the relationship was thereby redefined. Whatever you believe, how sexual attraction is resolved is fundamental to the survival of the friendship. When the attraction is acted upon, a romance may result. If sexual interest is not reciprocated, sometimes the relationship ends. In some cases, the sexual tension is contained or wanes over time and friendship can result.

So for many women, relationships with male friends just seem different than their friendships with other women. We believe, however, that our female friendships deserve some appreciation and examination whatever our experiences with male friends. We want to celebrate these very important relationships which do not seem to get much attention elsewhere.

Typically, other relationships in our lives receive most of our attention, such as lovers, spouses, children, and family members. It is easy for us to draw strength from our women friends to deal with these other relationships without taking the time to notice or appreciate what we've received. We can never repay the immeasurable debt we owe to these relationships, but we can pause for a moment and reflect on their importance to us. Here we have gathered stories to examine these friendships and honor these women.

Sharing Our Stories

When friends ask for a second cup they are
open to conversation. . . .

One of the most powerful ways women help define each other and our experience as women is through the simple joy of sharing our stories with each other. As with our female ancestors, women gather together to share our stories wherever and whenever we can—in the park while watching our kids, over a cup of tea, in the office in between appointments, at a favorite cafe, late at night on the phone. American poet Carolyn Kizer confesses, "women are the custodians of the world's best-kept secret: Merely the private lives of one-half of humanity."[14]

Sometimes our story sharing has been caricatured in the negative as "gossip." Women have, at times, been thereby shamed into isolation. Barbara Walters puts the kibosh on that notion when she says, "Show me someone who never gossips, and I'll show you someone who isn't interested in people."[15] By telling our stories, we learn about relationships. These stories tell us how to treat each other—what is acceptable, what is honorable, and what is not.

Telling our stories to other women creates an experience and understanding of feminine journeys that talking with men cannot achieve. Marilyn, one of the women we interviewed, explained, "Relating to my women friends makes me feel more intensely woman—not merely female but womanly. So much comfort, so sane. Men are not calming to me, but of course that doesn't matter because my girlfriends are."

One of the reasons telling our stories to women is so satisfying is that, in general, women listen and support each other emotionally and spiritually. We give to each other something required for us to keep our bearings—connection to the unique challenges of womanhood. We risk being known when we tell other women about ourselves. As Harriet Braiker writes, "It's entirely in your power to regulate the degree to which you peel back the layers of your personality when you disclose yourself to someone. You can keep that person on the surface, or you can allow her to penetrate, by degrees or directly, to the core."[16]

With our girlfriends, we peel back many layers of our personalities. This process is an intimate and, we believe, sacred undertaking. Anyone who has shown that willingness to expose their darkest secrets or greatest fears to another woman understands the treasure of a trusted girlfriend. We do not feel that the use of the term *girlfriend* denigrates that solemnity, although a few women we spoke with expressed concern about using the term. Somewhere in the past, this word has become associated with the trivial, the inconsequential. We don't think so, and we officially, here and now, reclaim the word to describe our best, our crucial friendships.

Our friendships with our girlfriends have a life cycle all

their own. Relationships are birthed; they mature, grow, and eventually end. To reflect the cycle of friendship, we have grouped the stories we've collected into five areas: Discovering Friends, Sharing Girlhood Adventures, Savoring Friendship, Outlasting Transition, and Remembering Friends.

Sometimes our friendships coincide with our life cycles, and we can draw on the support of these friends throughout our entire lives. Other friendships last for a shorter period of time, emerging and blossoming in a particular situation or era of our lives. Whether a friend travels with us for a short leg of the journey, for years, or for a lifetime, our bonds to other women can serve as a source of comfort, wisdom, and direction and shape the women we become. Join us in sharing the precious stories women told us about their loves, adventures, losses, triumphs, mistakes, celebrations and laughter — of their unique yet common experiences of being women. Experience with us the joys of becoming who we are and naming ourselves, starting with calling each other "girlfriends."

Faces of Friendship

The shared memories brought smiles, laughter,
a few tears and, at last, a sense of contentment.
For slowly, from our treasured memories
a kindred bond began to emerge.

That's how it is with people sometimes.
When you least expect it, a common thread —
golden, at that — begins to weave together
the fabric of friendship.

— MARY KAY SHANLEY

She Taught Me to Eat Artichokes:
The Discovery of the Heart of Friendship

Discovering Friends

And we find at the end of a perfect day,
The soul of a friend we've made.

—CARRIE JACOBS BOND

In many ways there are similarities between becoming
friends and finding a romantic love. Just as there can be
love at first sight, so a friendship can click in the blink of an
eye. Other friendships grow and show themselves in time,
similar to finding that you are in love with someone you
have known a long while. Whatever the circumstances,
every woman seems to remember when she found her girlfriends—that first moment she recognized a special friendship.

Instant Recognition

You meet your friend, your face brightens —
you have struck gold.

KASSIA (c. 840)

Sometimes, when we least expect it, we identify a soulmate in a flash. Without explanation, we understand each other, as if we've known each other before we met. Such was the experience of Meredith, a South African woman, who was having lunch one day with her boyfriend when she discovered Elaine, a woman who would become one of her closest friends. Elaine waited on their table and recognized Meredith's accent. Meredith was delighted to find that Elaine had spent several years in South Africa. After the two women excitedly exchanged phone numbers, Elaine warned, "You had better phone me soon!" Meredith laughed, "Listen to this woman! She already has a hold on me!" Which of course, she did, and they are best friends (although an ocean apart) to this day.

Even young girls can recognize a potential friend in an instant, as Kathleen, a learning specialist, told us. She described how she first recognized a friend in Mary when they were both just ten years old and living in a working-class neighborhood in Pittsburgh. "When Mary was first introduced by the head nun to our fifth grade class, I knew immediately she was someone special. First, because she was the only girl there who wasn't Caucasian. Mary is

Chinese, from a highly educated family—both of her parents had doctorates in medical research—and the rest of us were either Polish or Italian and from working-class families. All of us were curious about her because nobody moved into this neighborhood. You were born there and lived there forever unless you managed to get out.

"But what really struck me about her was how confident she was. A few minutes into the class, the nun was talking about China and Mao Tse Tung. Mary's hand shot up and she said to the nun, 'That's Mao Tse Tung' in this perfect Chinese dialect. Well, no one ever contradicted a nun—I mean, you didn't even look at them directly; when a nun walked into the room you stood up. We were shocked! Who was this person?

"She did it again the next day. When the class took turns doing recitals on Friday, she came up and did this unbelievable classical piano piece. She was this shining star and also someone who would stand up to these ridiculous nuns. I just fell in love with her. Here I was, very browbeaten and hating school. I would sit in the back of the class and read and plot to get out. Mary had a visible intelligence; she was poised, funny, and beautiful. We have remained friends for thirty-six years—since we were ten—and have never missed sending birthday cards to each other in all that time."

For Kathleen, the characteristic that distinguished Mary was her confidence. For Marilyn, a jewelry designer in New York, it was enthusiasm that initially attracted her to her best friend, Victory. "My husband and I took a walking tour that started at Vincent Sardi's restaurant in the theater district in New York and proceeded down through Hell's Kitchen. My husband made quite a few jokes about 'this little person,' one of the women who was walking behind us. I immediately liked her enormously because she was even more enthusiastic than I. I felt that anyone with that much curiosity was bound to be interesting and a great friend. And she was.

"We saw this extraordinary club, a yacht club with the entire stone exterior done to look like the prow of a ship going through water. The club didn't permit women to join—this was in the midseventies—and women could only go at certain hours. Due to her perseverance and negotiating talent, Vicki was able to arrange an appointment. And I said, 'Well, if you're going, I'm going!' So we made plans to have lunch at this place. When we went, I had a bit of a disaster when I realized I had left my purse in the cab with five hundred dollars in it. Miracle of miracles, the cab driver brought my purse back, saying he hadn't even looked inside. I was so grateful. It was a bonding experience and from that moment on, Vicki and I became very good friends, fast friends. And she's now been in my life for over two decades!"

Perhaps we are drawn by shared travels and life experiences, like Meredith and Elaine, by the offering of hope during a dark time of life, as Kathleen received from Mary, or the camaraderie of surviving an adventure, like Vicki and Marilyn. No matter what sparked that first moment of recognition, most of us have made a friend in one day — women we hold close to our hearts every day of our lives.

Mirrors of the Soul

The depth of a friendship — how much it means to us . . . depends, at least in part, upon how many parts of ourselves a friend sees, shares and validates.

—LILLIAN RUBIN

Our mothers told us that we should wait for the right man to come along. But few told us that we may have to wait for the right women friends as well. How do we recognize these women? What is the common characteristic that distinguishes our closest and best friends from our acquaintances? The answer seems to be, in part, that they mirror who we are.

For example, Nancy, a real estate broker, counted off the adjectives that best describe her girlfriends: "Honest, loyal, nonjudgmental, have a sense of humor, smart, and function from the heart, instead of being calculating." Nancy didn't realize that she had just described herself! Like Nancy, we all may have a difficult time acknowledging that we possess those valuable qualities we admire in our friends.

Sue Bender, author of *Plain and Simple*, and Mitzi McClosky, a therapist, discovered each other at a four-session cooking class conducted by a mutual friend. Mitzi told us, "Neither of us was very interested in becoming a gourmet cook. We were just there to support our talented friend and to have a good time." Sue continued, "By the end of the sessions, Mitzi and I had discovered that we were fellow spirits. We both like being rambunctious, irreverent—we were giggling in all the same places—and a little ornery and that made it fun for us to be together."

We asked Michiko, a forty-two-year-old artist, how she knows when an acquaintance might become a close friend. She replied, "That's a little bit mysterious. I try to discern if she is trustworthy. Also, I see whether we seem to perceive each other in a way that's comfortable to each other. I think when you chronically misperceive someone or they chronically misperceive you, that's usually something that you almost can't get around. You can't get really close."

Intuition can play a part in recognizing a girlfriend, as Carolyn, a government attorney, told us. "Twice, I've had a strong feeling that someone would be a close friend before I actually met her or spoke with her in person. Both times I had seen her in a class or meeting and may have heard her speak but had had no personal contact. Both times that person became a very close friend."

It can be exciting to find someone similar to ourselves. We feel like we've found a long-lost friend even though we've only just met. Some women described such an immediate bond as a connection meant to be. Perhaps we call out to one another from the deepest parts of ourselves for an intimacy that is possible only between women of like souls and minds.

Thrown Together

But every road is tough to me
That has no friend to cheer it.

—ELIZABETH SHANE

Life frequently throws us into transitions that create an openness to new friendships we might not have if life were moving along smoothly and predictably. Facing unfamiliar circumstances, new expectations, and the loss of former supports can engender a need for someone new to come into our lives. Such was the experience of Nancy, a forty-year-old corporate officer, who told this story, "I first met Lisa at a party. I had just moved to San Francisco after college, partly because my boyfriend lived here and partly because I wanted to move to California. It was scary because I felt I was going into his territory. I hardly knew anyone at this party, and I was not used to introducing myself to large crowds of people. Lisa immediately introduced herself and started asking me questions about myself, making it clear that she was interested in getting to know me as a person independent of my boyfriend. I thought, 'Oh, this is what I need.' I will never forget how grateful and relieved I felt. Here she was in a very comfortable situation—she had grown up with this group of people—and I was in an uncomfortable one. Lisa made room for me, a new person, in her life and let me be myself."

Lisa's instinctive recognition of Nancy's uncomfortable situation and her generous response made Nancy feel welcomed as an individual and helped put her at ease. Lisa continued her support as she helped Nancy find an apartment and shared her knowledge of the city with her. Twenty years later, Nancy has never forgotten her friend's sensitivity and friendship.

Sometimes a shared and traumatic transition can turn strangers into close friends. The empathy created by sharing emotional experiences can be like a fast-drying glue to a new friendship. Whether a friend shares our feeling or merely understands it, her ability to make room for our emotion is invaluable. Especially when we share our tears, the comfort offered in those moments of vulnerability, the swollen-eyed, red-nosed openness, can mark the beginning of loving friendship. Sharon, a recent college graduate, had this story: "I had just moved into the dorms my freshman year in college. I was nervous and scared, not just about being at college, but about meeting my roommate. I had always lived alone, and I didn't know how I would handle living with someone, especially if this someone was a stranger. I also missed my ex-boyfriend, with whom I had just broken up that morning.

"When I got to my room, I could tell that my roommate had already moved in. She had left a note saying she had gone to the Grateful Dead concert and would be returning later. I just sat there thinking about my ex-boyfriend, my friends, and everyone at home. When my roommate, Holly, finally came home, she found me sitting at my desk crying my eyes out. It must have been a shock to her. After I told her why I was crying, she let me know that she understood and that she had just said good-bye to her boyfriend and wouldn't be seeing him for a while. It really helped me to know that someone else knew what I was going through and that she didn't think I was foolish for crying on my first night at college. Eventually Holly and her boyfriend split and I reconciled with my boyfriend and then split up again, but Holly and I remained very good friends. It seems our friendship outlasted our relationships with the men we thought we'd never get over."

The experiences of Nancy and Sharon illustrate how a friendship can grow in times of transition, crisis, and change. Even though we have just met, these new friends seem to understand our insecurity and need for comfort and guidance. They give us a sense that we are perceived as we really are. In response to being known, our muscles untense, we breathe more deeply, we are relaxed. We somehow know it is safe to trust and rest in a new friendship.

Eyecatchers

Two may talk together under the same roof for many years,
yet never really meet; and two others at first speech
are old friends.

—MARY CATHERWOOD (1899)

In any given day, we may come into contact with dozens of women, most of whom pass by us unnoticed. What sets a potential friend apart from the crowd? What about her catches your eye? We asked women these questions and found out that what got their attention was frequently something noteworthy in the eyes of their new friends.

Such was the case for Jill, an English instructor, who recognized a potential friend by the quality of eye contact between them when they met. "I didn't presume that we would be good friends, but I knew the potential was there because of the way she looked at me while we talked. She had a penetrating, intimate stare—not one that was intimidating, but rather one that expressed genuine interest. I think it is harder for some women to accept a stare of that nature from a man because of the sexual undertones that can generally accompany it. However, I think that we women want to know that what we are saying or sharing is important, and we constantly seek nonverbal clues—eye contact, body language, and facial expressions—to tell us how we are affecting the ones to whom we are talking."

Robin, a psychotherapist and ordained minister, recognizes new friends by the quality of their eye contact. "I watch to see how comfortable they are with me. I think it's a confidence I'm looking for. I connect with women who are educated or love books, love reading, are on a growing edge, love travel, or are gutsy. I guess I identify with women who take risks and try things that don't always work. If a person isn't intense, then I get bored." Robin looks for that intensity in the eyes of her new friends.

Nina, a psychotherapist from southern California, spotted a potential girlfriend in a classroom of faces during graduate school. Nina told us, "I walked into class and saw her. There was something special about the look in her eyes, and I thought she looked like someone I wanted to get to know. Later I saw her on campus, and I introduced myself and asked if she'd like to go to lunch. A couple of days later, we went out together and talked for four hours, getting refills of Diet Cokes. I knew that day that she would be a lifelong friend. She now lives in Vermont and I in California. Through the transitions, we've retained a fabulous relationship. In fact, we call each other every other Sunday, taking turns calling. But at that first lunch, it was an intuitive thing. I just knew we'd be close friends."

For Carolyn and Michelle, law students, it wasn't the quality of their eye contact but the quantity that brought them together. Although they had the same class schedule, it was their remarkably similar bladder schedules that prompted their acquaintance. When they kept running into

each other in the restroom, they finally introduced themselves, as they obviously had so much in common!

We often hear the phrase "the eyes are the mirrors of
the soul." Like Robin, the intensity or confidence in a
woman's eyes may draw us to her, or the openness of her
gaze may trigger a sense that she is trustworthy. Alter-
natively, the quantity of met glances may convince us that
we are fated to meet. If a woman catches our eye, we pay
attention—we may have found a new friend.

I Never Thought We'd Be Friends

*The growth of understanding follows an ascending spiral
rather than a straight line.*

—JOANNA FIELD

All strong friendships have chemistry, but what about those
relationships that start out explosively? Liza, a resource
teacher, met Miranda while back in college. She said, "The
campus was in disrepair, which is the kindest thing I can
say. We lived in units of four rooms that shared a bath. You
couldn't take a shower for more than thirty seconds before
the bottom was completely filled with water. Really gross.

"Miranda was in a different room, but in the same unit.
I surveyed my living quarters and all but went ballistic
about the bathroom. Miranda heard me complaining, and
she told me later that she was upset at the thought of spend-

ing the year with a whiner. She stormed around and then decided that the only way to handle this was to get with it. So Miranda went in and cleaned the bathroom, turning her anger at me into cleaning energy. When we started talking and laughing about it, we became friends. And we still are today, twenty years later!"

Occasionally, we discover a friend in someone to whom we had assigned a stereotype, and remarkably, stereotypes always seem to be negative. Georgia and Laurie, investment bankers at the time, nearly lost the chance to become friends when they both classified the other upon sight. Laurie retells the tale: "I had just moved to New York from California and started this job where I knew no one. I was unpleasantly surprised that no one had made an effort to get to know me. When Georgia and I met at the copy machine, I saw her as a stereotypical 'East Coast preppie' and she pegged me as your 'typical Californian.' Nevertheless, Georgia showed me how to use the copy machine. But best of all, she asked me to have lunch with her. We've been great friends ever since."

We not only have to avoid stereotyping, we may need to resist the temptation to take personally someone's communication style or attach a specific meaning to a facial expression. Accurately reading the signals a prospective friend sends out is critical if a friendship is to begin. Pat, a program administrator, tells about the first time she met Renee, ten years ago when Renee started working at Pat's office. Pat said, "I'm not sure why, maybe it was the way she looked at me or something in her voice, but I got the immediate impression that she didn't like me. I couldn't figure out what I'd done, but I thought maybe I'd made some awful comment or something. But then one day, after I'd complained about something happening to me, she left a teddy bear by my door. I remember thinking, 'Wow, this is a big deal.' After that she invited me to a party, and then it finally dawned on me, 'Okay, she likes me!'"

Elise, a sales manager in her midthirties, said that after Leslie, a roommate whom she had met through a matching service, moved into Elise's apartment, "I wouldn't give an inch. I don't know how she lived with me, actually. When Leslie came to be my roommate, I remember having all these issues with her. I remember her buying all these new placemats and me curling my lip and shoving them in a drawer. She was so full of life, she would always say, 'Why don't you come hiking with me?' I would respond with, 'Honey, I like to sit in the café and write in my journal, and if I could smoke more cigarettes, I would. I don't want to go walk in nature.' Leslie would respond, 'Okay, fine.' The hilarious thing is that there was not one thing that she suggested I do with her that I didn't end up doing within the year. After the first year, it was a big lovefest all the time."

After their first meeting in the sorority they both joined, Susan, now twenty-seven, and Katherine, now twenty-five, would never have imagined that they would later become business partners *and* roommates. Susan says of Katherine, "I thought she was stuck up because she was quiet," and

Katherine says of Susan, "She was so loud and obnoxious at our first meeting, she wanted to know everybody's story!" After they graduated from college, they worked in retail and service industries and kept in touch through "girls' night out," which usually consisted of dinner or watching *Melrose Place*. As they got to know each other better, they both realized that they did not feel respected in their jobs or as customers when they were shopping. So they decided to start their own store, a place where women could go to "shop, hang out, and feel like we felt on our girls' night out." So they did, and two years later, they are best friends and their store in San Francisco is a success. But how could it not be—it's called girlfriends™!

I Always Wanted to Be Like Her

I believe that we are always attracted to what we need most, an instinct leading us toward the persons who are to open new vistas in our lives and fill them with new knowledge.

—HELENE ISWOLSKI

Friendships occasionally blossom because we admire another person. We sense that the more we know her, the more we may learn from her. Lillian Rubin points out in her seminal book on friendship, *Just Friends*, "Sometimes we choose a friend who mirrors our fantasies, dreams of a self we wish we could be."[1] Mary, a flight attendant based in Chicago, told us about a woman who impressed her upon first meeting and continues to influence her today: "A beautiful woman, Susan, is my best friend and guardian angel of eleven years. I met Susan as a rookie at an altitude of 31,000 feet, working on board an American Airlines DC-10 aircraft. Susan's spontaneous and infectious laugh caused my stomach to cramp as my tears of laughter dribbled to the floor. I decided that day that I wanted to be like Susan, or at least share a friendship.

"Through the years, Susan's generosity, kindness, and grace have continued to command my respect and admiration. She is steady and consistent with her decisions, and I always know that I can trust and rely on her. Susan's heart is worth millions in gold. For her, friendship is a natural, God-given talent. My best interest is always Susan's priority and never negotiable. I am grateful for Susan and her grace and generosity. She has helped me to learn and grow into a more caring human being."

As we mature, we may find ourselves drawn to women we perceive as different from ourselves—women who would have intimidated us or made us uncomfortable in previous times of our lives. This attraction may be a signal that we are developing a new aspect of ourselves. As Ms. Rubin points out, "For we are all more complex, with more varied traits and potentialities, then we know and can see."[2]

Patrice, a social worker, was immediately drawn to Yolanda the first day of a dance class they took together.

Patrice said, "She was everything I wanted to be—graceful, elegant, poised, and still open and warm. I usually feel a bit awkward and clumsy. But every move she made was like gliding through water. She smiled at me and so I went up to talk to her. She helped me out as we learned the dances. I'll always have my own style, but I enjoy learning things from her and modeling myself after her at times."

Sally, an executive secretary and painter, told us that she had always admired painters and other artists, but felt intimidated by them. She told us, "I would avoid going to any local art shows because I was afraid I'd meet artists! I loved looking at paintings but was in awe of painters and felt self-conscious around them. I was afraid they might ask me questions and discover my ignorance about painting!

"Then I met Ellen at a mutual friend's party, and didn't realize until far into our conversation that she was a painter—she actually supported herself as a professional artist. I felt so comfortable around her that I confessed my fear of artists. From then on, Ellen would take me to art shows, and explain different things to me about art. Now I've started doing my own painting, which Ellen has encouraged me to do. I realize that perhaps I was so intimidated because I desperately wanted to paint myself, yet was afraid of failure." Sally's story illustrates Ms. Rubin's observation: "A new friend, then, one who is different from us or from others in our life, is not the result of some random event or accidental meeting. Rather, this may be the first sign that we are ready to drop the defenses that have inhibited the expression of some part of the self, the first glimmering that some part not yet consciously known is ready to emerge. . . ."[3]

We may be choosing a friend because we admire her, and yet, in admiration, aren't we expressing who and what we would like to become? Perhaps we are ripe for some new growth, and our friend will facilitate that development.

She's as Crazy as I Am

What is exciting is not for one person to be stronger than the other . . . but for two people to have met their match and yet they are equally as stubborn, as obstinate, as passionate, as crazy as the other.

—BARBRA STREISAND

An easy confidence arises when we seem to know that someone we've just met will understand our bizarre sense of humor or stupid jokes. We can boldly say something ridiculous and not be embarrassed. When sixteen-year-old Vanessa Carlisle met her "zany, beautiful, artsy" friend Jessica, they were sitting next to each other in an art class at school. "I remember that we knew each other by name, but that was about all we knew of each other. We were working on a project that bored both of us. I picked up a piece of scratch paper and scribbled '*Why?*' on it. She turned it over and wrote, *'Because it's all your fault.'* I giggled and found a new piece of paper, and wrote, *'but, I want to know why!'* and thus started a very creative correspondence on bits of artwork and scrap paper.

"Every day in our class, in between brush strokes, we created strange situations and the matching wisdom to deal with them. We discussed my love life using images of fence posts, old eyes, and trees on fire and how sharp thoughts made up for dull pencils. We imagined societies where everyone appreciated themselves and their capability to be crazy. Many of the messages we wrote to each other were completely random phrases that had simply jumped into our minds at the time: *'Pebbles don't talk to boulders even though they are the only ones who know the secret.'* But we both understood them and loved finding the connections between them."

For Lucy, an eighty-six-year-old great-grandmother who has "finally decided to be a senior citizen," laughter initially created a barrier, then formed a central building block to an important friendship. "My best friend as an adult was Jane. She has said that we have been best friends for thirty years. I can't imagine it has been that long. We met at a luncheon at a women's club. She at once started talking about the difficulties of her divorce—her husband had left her for a mutual friend—and raising three young children on her own. She told stories about coming home and finding her car gone, and another time finding all the furniture gone. Well, it all sounded like a soap opera, and I laughed. She shook her finger at me and informed me that it was no laughing matter. I told her I knew that and asked if she would have lunch with me the following week. I was sure she felt she never wanted to see me again, but she came to lunch anyway. That was long ago, and we have been best friends ever since.

"She still does not know what to do with her three unmarried children, and she tells me all about it and I still laugh. Then she sees the humor and she laughs as well. I love her dearly, and in between her visits to me we have long telephone calls and laugh. She is so very good and caring about me. In 1994, she brought me home to Fresno after I had a serious bout with cancer and cared for me until she felt I could take care of myself."

What is funny for one person may make another shake her head in bewilderment. So, finding another woman who shares our weird, twisted brand of humor, who giggles at the same places, or who laughs to the point of tears when we do is a special gift. In fact, a shared sense of humor can lead to the "twin speak" that Sue Thoele, author of *A Woman's Book of Courage*, shares with her best friend, Bonnie Hampton, a psychotherapist. Bonnie told us about communicating with Sue: "Sometimes it almost feels like twin language, in that I will just say something, and she knows exactly what I'm talking about and she just screeches and thinks I'm hilarious. And it probably wasn't a bit funny to anyone else. It has to do with understanding each other's secret language. Understanding the metaphors. I could pull something out of some obscure book that I read; she may not have read the book, but she gets the metaphor, and that's fabulous."

Sharing a sense of humor lays the foundation for other, more difficult communication. When we asked Sue and Bonnie how talking to each other helps when one of them is feeling blue, Sue responded, "There are two things. First, it's to be really listened to. Second, it's the wit. In the most serious, most devastating moment, if there's a good line we both go for it. It's understood, and important, that you go for the good line. The grief and the joy are always all mixed up together. For me that's what makes the friendship so solid." Bonnie agreed. "I can call Sue and I can just be in a rage, and pretty soon I'm laughing. Or she's laughing at me. And that's the fabulous part of it."

The outrageous images of Vanessa and Jessica, Lucy's poking fun which annoys, then amuses her friend Jane, and Bonnie and Sue's refusal to pass up the good line are all ways we keep each other laughing. Being crazy together can pull us through the tough times. So enjoy the laughs, and give humor the honor it deserves. If we can keep each other laughing, we can keep each other sane.

Mistaken Identity

How desperately we wish to maintain our trust in those we love! In the face of everything, we try to find reasons to trust. Because losing faith is worse than falling out of love.

—SONIA JOHNSON

The friendships we value most are those that have a natural rhythm of give and take, shared vulnerability that is mutually beneficial to both women involved. However, sometimes what may look like a friendship, initially, turns out to be something else, something out of balance. Perhaps this woman is a mentor, a guide, or a caregiver but, sadly enough, she is not a friend. She does not have that unspoken appreciation of what we are experiencing, the ability to be there without being asked. And in that disappointment, we experience the sting of betrayal and regret.

One woman had this painful experience when someone significant in her life did not share her perception of the friendship: "She and I grew up together, and she was a part of my life well into adulthood. She was always one step ahead of me, it seemed. She was the person who led me to meditation. She's the one who introduced me to one of my best friends. She helped me get my first job when I got out of college. I realized later that I was projecting something onto this relationship that wasn't there.

"The wake-up call was painful. The only year that my child was alive, I didn't keep a diary, but I sent her letters

40

about my son when she was living out of the country. Those letters were my diary, and she threw them all away. I wouldn't have thought much about it, except when they moved back into the country they sent their household goods and stuff to our house and she sent back cartons full of spices—you know, cleaned out her cupboards and brought half-filled jars and stuff, but she had thrown away my letters. I was devastated, just devastated. And she said, 'Well, you don't know me, I don't keep things.'"

Barbara, an ad executive in her early thirties, tells of her experience as a teenager befriending Mari, an exchange student who turned out to be disloyal. Barbara told us, "I positively loved Mari. I was immediately attracted to her smile and warmth when we met, plus I knew she didn't know her way around, so I took her under my wing at school. Before long, however, I started getting this weird feeling about her, but nothing I could put my finger on. Rather than develop her own life, she sort of took over my life, spending her time with my friends. She even secretly dated my boyfriend! When I said anything to my friends about this, they thought I was just jealous. It was a very lonely and sad experience for me, because I felt betrayed by Mari and angry at my friends for being duped by her."

Most of us have made similar mistakes, thinking we have formed a unique bond with another woman, only to be disappointed. The woman appears to be a friend but just isn't. It may be tempting, after such a painful experi-ence, to hang up our spurs and retreat from taking any

41

more risks. But that course is an even bigger mistake. We all need other women in our lives, so, even though mistakes can hurt, they can also provide the wisdom to discern true friendship from false.

Opposites Attract

Each friend represents a world in us,
a world possibly not born until they arrive,
and it is only by this meeting that a new world is born.

—ANAÏS NIN

When we interviewed Melinda and Kim, friends for thirty-six years, they both commented on how different they are from each other and have been from their childhoods. First, they came from very different kinds of families. Kim explained, "Melinda's family was more professional class and mine more working class. My dad managed an auto parts store, and my parents paid cash for the house when they bought it—a big, old, drafty crackerbox house. Melinda, on the other hand, lived in a beautifully furnished, decorated house, having a dad with an office downtown. They had several cars—the black Olds, the VW, and the Datsun station wagon. This seemed like paradise to me."

When the girls reached junior high school, they went their separate ways for several years. Kim explained, "I was living life on the fringe. I moved to Madison, the big city, and I was a waitress in a doughnut shop, which for me had great political import. I unionized that doughnut shop, and, believe it or not, in 1971–72 that shop was underground central. I was living in a communal loft with about fifty other hippies. Melinda did the kind of direct, expected path with college, and I was doing doughnuts.

"Even though we are so different, we're still very close. We share a knowledge about our brothers and sisters and our mothers and fathers, of teachers, classes, classmates, places, things. As intimate as you can sometimes become in building a friendship as an adult, even then you can't capture that same sense of knowledge and understanding."

When Marilyn, a designer, was asked to describe her friend Victory, she described someone very different from herself. "Actually, we make a joke sometimes. We say that if the two of us were combined into one person we'd be perfect because of our very different skills." Asked to describe their differences, Marilyn responded, "She is much more analytical, while I process more intuitively. She is a great negotiator—extremely tenacious without appearing aggresive. I am exceedingly pragmatic—exceedingly. I love a sense of economy and prefer doing things in a nice, simple, direct, and quick way—maybe too quick. But not Vicki. She, on the other hand, always seems to have more time, more patience, and still gets it all done. She always has time, insight, and understanding enough for ten."

Robin, a psychotherapist and ordained minister, counts Reen, a woman she met in college, among her closest friends. Robin told us, "After college Reen moved to Missouri to a farm with her Mennonite husband, and they've lived in the same farmhouse for twenty-five years. They have three children, live a very simple Mennonite lifestyle, committed to world peace and the environment. On the other hand, in college, I was pro-Vietnam, voted Republican, and continue to be almost Reen's opposite. I've always lived in large cities, I'm single, have traveled internationally, and have two graduate degrees. And yet, once a year we come together, and we'll spend about thirty-six hours together. We stay up the whole night, talking and enjoying our rituals. I always bring a bottle of Ovaltine, and we make popcorn and talk all night long.

"We can be very different in terms of opinion, but, to Reen's credit, she's very tolerant. Her sense of herself is someone who learns, and she's always respectful of other people's opinions. We look for our common ground."

Sometimes we are attracted to women who seem quite different from ourselves only to later find that we have a great deal in common with them. Carmen, one of the authors, and Gail appeared to have little in common when they first met in Arizona while in graduate school twenty years ago. Carmen was from the West and Gail from the South; Carmen came from a conservative, sheltered home and was amazingly naïve for a woman in her twenties, while Gail was politically liberal, savvy, and more sophisticated. Carmen said, "At times I wondered what kept us together, especially after we both moved from Arizona and went our separate ways. But as the years have progressed and we've learned more about ourselves and each other, we've found that we have an amazing number of experiences in common. I treasure Gail because we share some similarities in our past and we're both tenacious, sarcastic, and somehow keep laughing through it all."

Commonalities? Differences? What brings us together and makes a relationship work? Maybe in some cases we find someone who, rather than insisting on *being like* us, is simply willing to *like* us—differences, similarities, warts, and all.

She Was There All Along

Real charity and a real ability never to condemn—the one real virtue—is so often the result of a waking experience that gives a glimpse of what lies beneath things.

—IVY COMPTON-BURNETT

Sometimes we don't recognize a friend until we have been circling in each other's orbit for a while. As Rene, a teacher from northern California, noted, "I met Cyndi when she and her husband came to pastor my church. We had, at first, a cordial relationship, exchanging a warm handshake and greeting every Sunday morning. It wasn't until we took some time one sunny autumn afternoon to have lunch that

I realized what a special friend Cyndi was going to be. There was something in the way we were able to open our lives to each other that was unlike anything I'd experienced before. I felt safe and accepted, and I couldn't believe how many life experiences and interests we had in common. There was an ease with which we shared together that felt like we'd been friends for a long time. I feel we will be friends always."

Laura, an attorney, learned an important lesson from a relationship that started out anonymously: "In high school, I was on a drill team with fourteen other young women. There was a week where we played 'secret angels.' We exchanged names, and whoever's name you had, you would just spoil that person anonymously every day for a week. We went through the first six days, and my 'angel' did all these great things for me. She left me all these treats and had this really uncanny knowledge of me—she always seemed to know the thing that I wanted that day—so I figured it had to be somebody I knew fairly well out of the group. The seventh day came, and we were supposed to exchange baby pictures on that day.

"Suddenly this girl named Andrea came to me. She was the person that I probably knew the least out of the group of friends. She was in tears, saying, 'I can't give you my baby picture because I'm Japanese and you'd know it was me.' It was the first time that I really had a chance to understand what it meant to be different. She was very quiet and never had told anybody that she felt different or odd in any way, so I was the only person who ever knew that secret about her. We became very close after that."

We perhaps don't see the depth of friendship until a moment of frightening vulnerability shakes a close friend out of the woodwork. When we interviewed Arlene Bernstein, author of *Growing Season*, we asked how the death of her first-born child changed her friendships: "Judy was always a close friend since college, but she showed a strength and caring I hadn't experienced prior to the day we went together to visit a friend in the hospital who had just had triplets. I wasn't expecting to have a problem with seeing the babies because I'd been in the hospital since my first baby had died. However, our friend's babies were preemies, and when I saw them in the incubator, I just fell apart. These three little creatures looked just like my first baby. I collapsed. Judy walked me around Golden Gate Park for about three hours, letting me cry and talk and talk and cry. Until then I had seen her as matter-of-fact, very private with her emotions, so not the person to go to with mine. This incident was the beginning of a new depth to our friendship that we have shared since that day."

There may be no connection between two women until they discover the common thread of their lives. Even though Sue, an author and artist and Mitzi, a therapist, are very close at this point, nothing had clicked when they had first met. Mutual friends had introduced these women to each other, suspecting they would enjoy each other, but the friendship did not take off right away. Sue said, "Though we were told we would like each other, and we were interested in the same things, I think we both just said, 'Hmmmm.' At the beginning we didn't see anything to connect with. We didn't see what the other had to offer."

Years later their friendship blossomed when Sue sponsored Warriors of the Spirit, a group for women in which Mitzi participated. Sue said, "I wanted to use the imagination. We used clay, we did fairy tales, body sculpting. I wanted to break down our regular, rational minds." Mitzi continued, "I felt Sue's expansive spirit and remarkable wisdom in that room from the start. Soon after the first class, we had lunch together, and our relationship has deepened ever since."

We may feel the pull of a true friend right away, or the tie may be uncovered years later in some unexpected way. When we discover her is irrelevant. What matters is that she has become one of our nearest and dearest, and we cherish her friendship no matter when it deepens.

Sharing Girlhood Adventures

Gentle ladies, you will remember till old age what we did together in our brilliant youth!

—SAPPHO (c. 600 B.C.)

Remember the games we played? Catherine remembers playing hopscotch with her best friend, Jane. How about the thrill of adventure? Allison and her friends would steal lemons from their neighbors' yards to make lemonade and sell it on the street corner. Sometimes we scared ourselves to death; Katie remembers playing "I believe in Mary Worth" in the dark of night at slumber parties, where each girl would stare at a mirror and recite that phrase, with the belief that a bloody and haggard Mary Worth would appear after one hundred repetitions. (Katie said that no one ever made it that far, however, without bursting into giggles or screaming and running from the room.) Just the excitement of wheedling our parents to let us spend time with our friends was a breathless, high-stakes exercise of anticipation. Helen summed it up with her example: "I would beg permission to stay over at Mary's. When I finally received it, I would run along the dark city streets of Pittsburgh until I reached her house, climb up the many steps to her front door and then three further flights to her bedroom. We would change into white nightgowns, listen to classical music, eat potstickers, and play word games." Ahhh, satisfaction.

We can tell friends we meet now *about* our childhoods, but the girlfriends we made in our youth shaped our childhoods. The girlfriends who shared our "firsts" as we grew from toddlers into teens powerfully influenced the direction our lives would take. Rosemarie Lennon, in her article, "Childhood Friends Shape Our Lives Forever," claims that these girlfriends helped "mold our personalities, form our characters and determine who we are today." She writes, "If your friends were kind, caring and supportive, it's likely they fostered in you a trusting and compassionate nature. On the other hand, if you were bullied or betrayed by your childhood pals, you may have grown up either shy and timid, or the experience may have toughened you into a fiercely independent woman."[4]

What childhood adventures shaped your development? We all have treasured (and not-so-treasured) memories of our youthful years.

Please savor the girlhood stories that have been shared with us. These stories may help us all remember the particular girls and adventures which shaped us as individuals.

Running with the Pack

*No matter by which culture a woman is influenced,
she understands the words 'wild' and 'woman' intuitively.*

—CLARISSA PINKOLA ESTÉS

Girlhood is a time to experiment with new activities, explore mysteries of life, and discover who we are. We find out what we like and don't like, who we think is funny, and what is fascinating or boring. Lida, a songwriter in her sixties, remembers, "Junior high was my time of 'running with the pack,' only our pack was giggling thirteen year olds whose worst escapade was smoking the sample cigarettes Jeannie's dad kept in the glove compartment of his car. My special best friend was Caryl. Her parents owned a small grocery shop with their living quarters above and behind the grocery room. They allowed us to have slumber parties where we had the entire second floor all to ourselves. It was the closest I'd ever been to being rich! We would play records, sing, talk about boys, laugh, and take innumerable pictures of one another—narcissistic little beasts that we were! We didn't know exactly who we were and needed the pictures to prove our existence, I think.

"To be really daring, we would sneak down the stairs and out of the house and boldly walk down the dark streets in our (gasp!) pajamas! The mission was to not get caught. The headlights of a car three blocks away would throw us into spasms of muffled giggles, and we'd fall all over ourselves trying to hide. Usually the car would turn before reaching us, but we'd feel the thrill of having won. It was a great time to be young!"

Packs can become especially important when we attain that brass ring of adolescence, the beloved driver's license. Many of us, especially those of us who grew up in small towns, can remember "cruising"—begging our parents for the car, then driving up and down the streets, exhilarated by our new freedom and mobility. Pamela, now a thirty-five-year-old attorney, remembers cruising with her friend Wendy. "Wendy, the youngest of three girls, and I, who had no sisters, kept a close eye on what Wendy's older sisters were doing. I was fascinated by how her sisters would fix their hair, what records they were listening to, who their boyfriends were. Sometimes we, new adolescents, would be allowed to ride along as one of her sisters went cruising with her friends—the ultimate grown-up activity. And as our sixteenth birthdays approached, we eagerly anticipated 'our turn' at the wheel of the family Impala—cruising up Main Street, and cutting over to Broadway to cruise downtown again. What excitement."

Bernadette, a professor, describes her teenage pack of girlfriends, on a night out on their own. "My high school friends and I had a 'girls' night out,' and I volunteered to drive on the assumption my parents would let me drive their car—the plusher, larger, more expensive one with the radio. However, my parents flatly refused, so I had to drive our tiny, beat-up Mazda with frayed upholstery and no radio. Each of my four friends gave me an amused grin as she crammed into my little car.

"On our way to the pizza parlor, someone hollered, 'Hey, Bernie, turn on the radio!' When I informed her there wasn't one, I was met with some disappointed groans and silence. However, a few seconds later, my friend said cheerfully, 'Well, I guess we will have to provide our own entertainment!' Then she burst into song. My other friends joined in — very loud, very obnoxious, and very out of tune. They tried to dance but began to knock each other with their elbows. I was so embarrassed I could hardly drive. After a light turned green, I forgot to put the car in first gear, trying instead to start in third. The car lurched violently through the intersection as my friends screamed and laughed. It was one of the most enjoyable times I had ever spent with those girls. They had made the most of what must have seemed like a disastrous situation."

Some things we do with our girlfriends may seem unbelievably silly to everyone else but are enormously funny to us. Trying to explain these activities may not work, for the incidents may make no sense to anyone else. But they do to our friends and us because at a moment in time our imaginations intersected. Asked why we did what we did, we can say only, "It seemed like a good idea at the time."

Rene, now in her forties, describes how she and two of her friends survived finals week in college: "We gathered up all the soda bottles we could find. Then we lined them all up and filled them with water, getting the notes just so.

Here were the three of us, lying on the floor, blowing 'Blue Danube' on soda bottles. It was a hoot! Literally!

"Another time we went to the laundry rooms, padded the bottoms and tops of the dryers with blankets, and got inside them. Sitting with our legs crossed, we could go around and around. Two or three revolutions were about all we could handle. But we had a ball for ten cents!"

We love the image of packs of girls, some just reaching puberty, some well into womanhood, scuttling about in search of enjoyment (although we don't recommend climbing into a dryer and starting it). The pack keeps us balanced, allowing us to dare to do new things we would not do alone, yet provides us with the safety net of shifting back into childhood and immaturity when we are not feeling so brave. We never outgrow the need for the wildness of girlhood or the allure of running with the pack. So do something wild with your girlfriends!

Childhood Commitment

The balm of life, a kind and faithful friend.

—MERCY OTIS WARREN (1776)

We learn as we grow how to deal with human relationships. Childhood friendships teach us what is considered good or unacceptable, which interactions foster commitment or disloyalty. Cosby Rogers, a Virginia-based developmental psychologist, asserts, "Our childhood friends were the first people to influence us outside our immediate family. When we peeked out into that big world beyond our front door, there they were. And the lessons we learned during those first encounters were powerful enough to last a lifetime."[5] These lessons include the pains and pleasures of attachment and commitment to other fallible human beings.

Wynn, now in her midthirties, learned the art of being dedicated to someone even when the going wasn't easy through her experience with her childhood friend: "My most enduring friendship is with my friend Karen, whom I have known for thirty years. Our mothers introduced us at age five when my family moved into Karen's neighborhood, a quiet suburb in northern California. Although we were initially cool toward each other—probably reluctant to satisfy our mothers' expectations that we would become fast friends—by age eleven we were inseparable. What set Karen apart at age eleven was her boldness and her sense of humor. I thought she was the funniest person alive. I admired her wit, intelligence, and her ability to challenge authority. At a time when I would have been characterized as a 'perfect student' type, she was the 'class clown.'

"Beginning in junior high and continuing through high school graduation, Karen and I rode our bicycles to school together every single school day. I believe this was my first experience with commitment. There were days when we were angry with each other or didn't want to even see each other, and yet in our unspoken way, we were committed to going to school together every day. There just wasn't any alternative. It would have been an unspeakable violation of trust not to have bicycled together, and so we did, five days a week, September through June, for six years.

"Although we attended different colleges and lived in different parts of the country, we continued to be the best of friends. Over the years, we haven't always made the same decisions about our lives, but we've gone through the major events together: higher education, thwarted romances, traveling abroad, first jobs, soul-searching, marriages, career changes, morning sickness, raising daughters, and an assortment of other triumphs and challenges. We have delighted in each other's successes, laughed about the human condition, taken each other's sides against real and imagined enemies, and coached each other through demanding times. When she asks, 'What can I do for you?' I know I can give her an honest answer and that she'll deliver on her promise."

The art of commitment that we learn in youth serves us well in our adulthood. Circumstances have required an adult level of commitment from some girls and young women. Catherine, a retired teacher now in her eighties, talks about the friendship that she shared with Lorraine: "My best friend and I met in first grade. In elementary school, I sat behind her, but I could not see the board, so Lorraine would write the test questions that were written on the board and pass them back to me on a piece of paper.

The teacher thought I was cheating, because nobody realized I couldn't read what was written on the board. The teacher had my mother come into school, and after Lorraine explained, they got eyeglasses for me." Who knows how Catherine's life might have been different had her friend not stood up for her. Without learning to read, Catherine would not have been able to get the level of education required to become a teacher. As it was, she taught first grade for thirty-five years.

Racial differences also put their friendship to the test. Because Catherine was black and her friend Lorraine was white, they faced the challenge of others' prejudices. Catherine told us, "Lorraine's father came from France and her mother from England, and they didn't mind my being friends with her. But others gave us trouble. For instance, we walked to school every day together, but the elementary school principal, who was very prejudiced, said that we shouldn't walk together and kept trying to prevent us from doing so.

"After high school, we went in different directions, but we remained friends the whole time she was alive. We just didn't let things like that stand in our way. I got married, but she didn't. My children called her Aunt Lollie, and they gave her presents and she gave them presents. She taught in the school for the deaf, and I taught first grade. We remained friends for decades, and it was just a lovely friendship. It didn't seem unusual to us because we just lived the whole way through it."

Wynn and Karen, Catherine and Lorraine have benefited throughout their lives from the rock-solid trust that began in childhood. Most of us have been similarly affected by girlfriends who taught us about faithfulness and loyalty. Such childhood friendships provided us with a stable foundation upon which we have built our own integrity and our ability to say to another woman, "You can count on me."

She Is Always with Me

Are we not like two volumes of one book?

—MARCELINE DESBORDES-VALMORE (1872)

Occasionally a girlhood friend affects us at such a deep level that we carry her mark and remember her love well into adulthood. Nan, a forty-year-old attorney, recalls the moment she spotted her first friend: "Lisa and I met when we were three years old. I was sitting on the front steps of my house with my mom, and Lisa, her mother, and her sister walked down the street. They had just moved into the neighborhood and had invited me to come down to see their new kittens. It was my first interaction with the outside world, and Lisa was the first person I remember that was my size. It was so exciting to go to their house; it was like going to a foreign country would be now. I can remember what their house looked like and what it smelled like, how it was different from my house. I even remember what they were wearing! Lisa and I were best friends all through grade school and high school, and then she went to college on the East Coast, while I went to Colorado. As soon as I got there, I missed her so much that I used my book money to buy an airplane ticket and flew to Vermont to surprise her. I just got on a plane and landed in Middlebury and wandered around until I found the college! We have lived very different lives, and yet we will always be good friends. She will always be a part of my life."

Jordan, now in college, still feels the pain of separation from her high school best friend, Kelly: "Kelly and I first met on Halloween. In the dark of that spook-filled niche of San Anselmo, Kelly ambled toward me in a chicken outfit that would make Big Bird jealous. Stuck somewhere inside that bulky chicken suit was a person who would share the majority of my high school years and leave me with a hollow ache as we got older—as well as an unconditional love, admiration, and respect for a person who continues to flourish.

"Kelly and I were like two parts of one person. She, the studious, silent intellectual type; athletic, always getting MVP on any team she was a part of, acing her classes and exams. Kelly was full of an energy, a wisdom, that would find its way out between the cracks and spread a diffuse light on anyone in her presence. I was the outgoing, the passionately rebellious, the poet who would sit with her for hours in the park as we discussed the rottenness of being teenagers. She became my muse and my confidant.

"We had plenty of adventures. She and I hiked in Deer Park almost every other day after school or on the weekends. We even hiked in our bras once, blushing as unsuspecting hikers rounded the corner past us.

"When Kelly and I both moved on to college, there was a shocking sense of disconnection that occurred, the painful wrenching of our deeply forged ties being slowly pulled apart. She would write to me of the wide and wonderful world where she had now found a niche, saying how sad it was to feel the distance. I can still feel the tears hot on my face. She will always be with me."

Even if our lives take unexpected turns and we are separated by time or geography from those women who shared our childhoods, we never lose the impact they have had on our lives. We take these girlfriends with us each and every day, in our memories as well as in the warp and weft of our personalities. The pain of separation subsides as we realize these friends are a permanent part of ourselves and our lives.

Bad Girls

I can sometimes resist temptation, but never mischief.

—JOYCE REBETA-BURDITT

In spite of the stereotype that little girls are made of "sugar and spice and everything nice," we women know that we made quite a bit of mischief when we were younger. Of course, some of us are still continuing in that tradition. Being bad is definitely part of being a girl, and women tell some amusing stories about childhood mischief with girl-friends.

Susan, a travel agent from New York, told us, "My most remembered friendship and trauma as a little girl was in the third grade. Sue, Sally, and I were best friends, playing together at recess. We tended to wait until the last minute to join the line so that the teacher had to announce that she would close and lock the classroom door. If you found it closed, you were to go to the principal's office and report yourself tardy—a fate that would mark you for life as a bad person. Sure enough, one day the class vanished inside without our noticing, and the dreaded door was closed.

"After quick consultation, the three of us decided to hide in the girls' bathroom until the bell rang to dismiss school, then retrieve our coats from our lockers and head for home as if we'd been in our assigned seats all along. We stood on the toilet seats so that Mrs. Welsh, the principal, wouldn't find us when she came to look for us. What messed up our plan was impatience.

"Fearing that someone would notice we were at the lockers after not being in class, we decided to retrieve our coats before the bell and then depart directly from the bathroom when the bell rang. We got about three steps outside the bathroom door on that mission when Mrs. Welsh rounded the corner in total panic because three third grade girls were missing.

"Her joy at locating us did not overcome her rules of punishment. We were each paddled with the highly varnished wooden paddle accepted in those days. Mostly, we suffered bruised pride and the stigma of having been so bad as to skip school. Sue and I have continued our friendship and still correspond to this day, even though I haven't seen her in twenty-five years. Our traumatic experience will be a bond to death."

Causing trouble is a favorite activity for young women as well as girls. Rene informed us, "In my dorm, we had a problem with ants and roaches. But the powers that be would do nothing about them. We kept complaining to the head resident, but nothing happened. So we thought we could convince her to act by gathering up as many live cockroaches as we could and letting them go under her door.

"We put the paper sack under her door, and they all went scurrying across the floor. Fifteen or twenty seconds later we heard this bloodcurdling scream, and the little old head resident, who had been there for years, came streaking out of her room screaming. She got on the phone and got those maintenance guys there. Those bugs were gone!"

Trisha told us she had friends in college who tried to play a trick on her, only it turned out to her advantage. She said, "I was a dorm resident assistant, and some of the girls in the dorm put an ad in the school newspaper saying, 'Lonely resident assistant needs date for the dance.' I didn't know they had done this and was totally at a loss when all these guys approached me saying, 'Gee, I didn't know you needed a date. If you'd have told me, I'd have taken you.' The great part is that I ended up going to the dance with Hugh, one of the guys who saw the ad. He became the love of my life—at least my college life. That joke worked out just fine for me!"

Causing trouble is great practice for when we are older. We learn to make up our own minds about rules, we learn the consequences of our actions, and we learn to defend ourselves. As Rene's story of the roaches so well illustrates, we may figure out some ways to beat the system, and as Trisha's story shows, we may be able to turn others' mischief to our advantage.

Would I Have Made It Without You?

I often think, how could I have survived without these women?

—CLAUDETTE RENNER

Looking back on childhood friendships caused some of the women we interviewed to realize just how important those friendships were in surviving difficult family situations. Layer upon layer of experiences teaches us about ourselves and one another. The burnishing and polishing of life's events creates a fine glowing vessel of friendship.

Cynthia, a grocery clerk in southern California, describes the richness that her lifelong friendship with Carmen has provided: "We have known each other since we were ten. We would see each other on Sundays at church and sometimes spend the afternoons together. I don't think we knew how dysfunctional our families were then. For me, being with her was fun, friendship, escape. I remember how we would laugh and have fun. I was a soprano and she an alto, so we'd play our guitars and make up songs. I still have copies of those songs. I got to do things with her and her family that my family never did. I remember spending Easter vacation in Palm Springs; I'll never forget that. We had so much fun by the pool flirting with the boys.

"The years went by; her family started going to a different church. We met up again in college. After college, we kept in touch by writing, phone calls, and occasionally meeting. For long periods of time we would not see each other, and yet when we met we would pick up where we left off. We gained a better understanding of each other as we gained a better understanding of ourselves, realizing the baggage we carried, trying to sort it all out as we lived our lives. Through all the years and phases, the bottom line is, we're friends, supporting each other through everything, every relationship, every parent, job, everything. We've not only loved each other but liked each other, and we still have fun when we're together. And we still sing."

Surviving difficult family situations can be tough, if not impossible, to do alone. Often we can look back and point to one or two friends who offered us an escape or a point of sanity along the way. Marla and Dierdre, now in their forties, wonder what they would have done without each other when they were young, dealing with families that were filled with conflict and confusion.

Dierdre explained, "Our families were very different, yet very similar. We both had many siblings, and sometimes things got a bit crazy at home. Marla and I created our own little world to escape the stress and angst of being prepubescent girls in large families. We made a playhouse that was our exclusive turf behind Marla's house. We created fantasy lives where we would reenact TV shows or pretend we were married adult women and our husbands did this or that. We used to camp out there. As I look back now I realize I relied heavily on my friendship with Marla to bring order and sanity into my life."

Marla added, "Dierdre and I would play for hours in her room too. She had a record player and 45s and lots of neat stuff. My bedroom was off limits even to me except for sleeping. The sanctity of Dierdre's room was comforting to me."

Dierdre summarized, "Our friendship as young girls taught me that sometimes you need to go outside of your family to get what you need. I knew I could rely on Marla. And although our methods of coping today are much different than when we were children, I still gain strength and peace of mind from our friendship. No one understands me the way Marla does. Today, because of our history together, a phone call or a simple nod from my friend can put things in perspective."

Dr. Tina Tessina, author of *True Partners: A Workbook for Developing Lasting Intimacy*, echoes this essential component of friendship. "Friends are incredibly valuable. Relationships with friends are usually less stressful than relationships with family or love interests and therefore more supportive."[6] Certainly in times of trouble, girlfriends with whom we create a safe and sane reality can be the thin thread that pulls us through.

Psssst. What About Sex?

Girlhood . . . is the intellectual phase of a woman's life, that time when, unencumbered by societal expectations or hormonal rages, one may pursue any curiosity from the mysteries of the yo-yo to the meaning of infinity. These two particular pursuits were where I left off in the fifth grade when I discovered a hair growing in the wrong place and all hell broke loose.

—ALICE KAHN

As Fannie Hurst was known to say, "Sex is a discovery."[7] Remember finding out from our girlfriends about boys and kissing and having periods and making babies? Remember the giggles and gasps of disbelief? Many of the women we interviewed described relying on their friends for this needed information. We may not have gotten accurate information, but asking our friends about sex wasn't quite as embarrassing as asking an adult.

Patty, a homemaker with a college-age daughter of her own, laughs when she recalls this experience: "Shirley, a close friend I met as a teenager, and I often laugh about a slumber party at the home of Susie, a mutual friend. Late that night, Susie quietly approached Shirley and me and asked quite seriously, 'When a boy kisses you, what side do you turn your head?' We still smile when we remember that serious face and that question."

Jenny spoke with a smile about her childhood alliance with Paula: "We did a lot of experimenting. We were boy crazy; we talked about boys and crushes, the Beatles. We each had our favorite Beatle."

Of course, there are the embarrassing questions of anatomy: what is so different about boys, and what in the world is going on in our own bodies? Jenny and Paula remember Paula's first experience seeing a grown man naked. Jenny said, "We were fifth graders and having a sleepover at Grandma Elsie's house. We were sneaking around, trying to spy on her roomer, George, or whatever his name was."

Paula blushes even now when she confesses, "I opened the door on him and he was completely naked. All I remember is that I was thoroughly traumatized. I just walked in and there he was, this adult man."

Jenny laughed, "I didn't witness it, but you came downstairs and told me the story. You were totally freaked out!"

Another important part of a girl's sex education is dealing with periods, pads, and tampons. Our own anatomical changes were explained to many of us by a flimsy film that eighth grade girls were herded into a room to see (causing great consternation and intense curiosity among the boys). The film made a rather halfhearted attempt to explain why having your period should not be considered "the curse." There was a lot of discussion about whether or not we could swim while we were menstruating, but none at all about the crucial details, such as how to actually install a tampon. This nitty-gritty information we had to glean from our girlfriends; we'd have rather died than ask our mothers about such matters. Mickey, an accomplished organist, told us this story: "I remember my girlfriend stood outside the bathroom stall, giving me step-by-step instructions about how to put in a tampon. Except she neglected to tell me to take the little tube out.

"I said, 'You know it feels like I just put a popsicle stick up me! Is it supposed to be this uncomfortable?'

"She responded, 'Just throw the tube away.'

"'Throw the tube away?' I queried.

"She said, 'Yeah, where is the tube?'

"'It's where the rest of it is!' I replied." Where else?

Guess who similarly provides those crucial details about sex? Our romantic partners owe our girlfriends tremendous gratitude (at least if the information they gave us turned out to be correct!). We gained that essential savoir faire through the sometimes reliable information bank of our friends.

Speechless

Silences make the real conversations between friends. Not the saying but the never needing to say is what counts.

—MARGARET LEE RUNBECK

A lot has been written, seriously and facetiously, about women's need for communication and talking. Yet, with a really good friend, frequently no words are necessary. Suzy, a poet and librarian in Connecticut, illustrated this with a story from those last days of her senior year in high school when everyone was signing yearbooks: "Karen and I exchanged yearbooks. My picture showed a round-cheeked young woman with glasses and a wistful look. Karen, also in glasses, looked thinner and more aquiline. I remember looking at her picture, and I couldn't think of anything to write. Here we were, best friends, emotional intimates. We'd been in a class together, had even gotten caught by the teacher for duplicating each other's home-work assignments, and no words would come. I looked at Karen and she at me. Simultaneously and silently we handed the books back to each other. It seemed more fitting to let them stay clean, unsigned, untied to that particular era of our lives. The open space itself symbolized our feelings about each other, that we would be in touch forever in a constant change that wouldn't be confined to the words below a Peter Pan-collar photograph."

A friendship sometimes *requires* not speaking. Everyone

has secrets—pieces of information that, out of fear or shame, we avoid telling anyone else. When a girlfriend feels close enough and safe enough to tell us such information, we are pleased and honored that we have won her trust. Frequently a woman lets another woman know that she is her most trusted friend by sharing an aspect of herself that she has kept secret from the rest of the world.

Amy tells this story about her friend Susan: "One night when we were still in high school, she came to my home in the middle of the night and woke me up by knocking on my window. I let her inside, and she was practically hysterical with tears, just sobbing and sobbing. I tried to calm her down, and she finally told me what was bothering her. Basically, she had decided to tell her current boyfriend something from her past that she had never shared with me. She felt bad 'cause she hadn't told me before and wanted to make sure that I knew before he did. I was really touched by how important it was to her." Sharing this confidence let Amy know she was Susan's most trusted friend.

At times, silence between friends is more eloquent than words. As illustrated by Suzy's and Karen's inability to find words to sum up their relationship, spoken language may not express the myriad of feelings, memories, and expectations of the future. Further, friendships may require that no words be repeated. Keeping silent is an expression of gratitude for a friend's having shared a valuable aspect of herself. In either case, being speechless has its own subtle meaning and value.

Roommates

Friendship is mutual blackmail elevated to the level of love.

—ROBIN MORGAN

As we changed from girls to young women, many of us learned how to navigate the big world with the assistance of roommates. Any relationship that survives living together, especially when we're young and sure we know everything about being grown-up, will probably be a long-lasting relationship.

Lynn, publicity director for a film studio, and Robin, a casting agent, shared living space with several different women after moving to San Francisco after college in the early 1980s. All of these women continue to be important components of one another's lives, although after hearing this story, it seems like a minor miracle! Lynn and Robin shared their story with us together.

Lynn moved in with Bridget, a college friend, and two other women, Robin and Sissy. Lynn began, "All four of us were living in this two-bedroom apartment, with Chloe, Robin's retarded cat. Bridget hated, hated cats. Of course, we weren't supposed to have four people in the apartment and we certainly were not supposed to have a cat.

"Sissy slept in the closet. Bridget lived in our dining room with no closet and had to put bamboo shades on the doorways. The cat could come under the shades, and Bridget couldn't touch the cat because she was scared of it.

And she would just yell at the cat, 'Get out! Get out!' She would sleep with a water bottle—it was like the old West, her gun by her side—and in the middle of the night, you could hear her scream and spray water at the cat. For some reason that cat loved to go into Bridget's room. Of course, Robin would lock her out of her own bedroom at night."

At this point Robin interjected with, "Well, I needed to sleep! I couldn't sleep with the door open. The cat had to be able to use the litter box."

Lynn continued, "Those of us lucky enough to have a bedroom would shut the door and the cat would try to get in by putting his paw under the door. It would be like *The Shining*, you'd hear this swishing sound.

"But one Saturday morning," Lynn went on, "the landlord called to see if he could come over to fix the stove or something. Sissy pleaded, 'Oh, uh, could you wait for an hour?' Immediately, we started dismantling the place so he wouldn't find out who and what was living there. Someone was sneaking the cat out, we were taking down the dining room cum bedroom, we were shoving everything into our cars, and so forth. We thought we were being quite clever.

"Well, it turned out the landlord came early, and he was sitting outside across the street watching this whole moving operation take place."

Robin smiled, "We were kicked out the next day. He was not amused."

We rather gingerly asked what they did after they had been kicked out of the apartment. Did they all move somewhere else? Were they able to find a place to accommodate all of them and a cat?

Lynn responded, "We all split up, actually."

Whereupon Robin reminded her sarcastically: "No, not all of us split up."

Lynn sheepishly realized her mistake: "Oh, that's right," she laughed. "We made Robin live on the other side of the street because of Chloe. We kicked her out!"

"Yes," Robin replied wryly. "My dearest friends, *all* of them, managed to find a flat together."

So, aren't roommates great? They can be our greatest supporters and most irritating companions, and they provide maximum fun. Oh, and they can keep us humble, too. Seems like a fairly efficient package. A priceless one as well.

Savoring Friendship

Love is like the wild rose-briar;
Friendship like the holly-tree.
The holly is dark when the rose-briar blooms,
But which will bloom most constantly?

—EMILY BRONTË (1846)

While meeting a new friend can be exhilarating, the most rewarding aspect of friendship is that day-to-day (or decade-to-decade) presence, whether it be immediate or distant. As friendships deepen and mature, we can take comfort that our girlfriends appreciate our support and are not offended by our bad moods or scared by our tears. We can settle into the friendship as into old slippers—remembering, of course, not to take even old slippers for granted. The dozens of women we interviewed spoke of their appreciation for and enjoyment of the following aspects of their friendships.

Loyalty

A friend doesn't go on a diet because you are fat. A friend never defends a husband who gets his wife an electric skillet for her birthday. A friend will tell you she saw your old boyfriend — and he's a priest.

—ERMA BOMBECK

There's nothing that warms the heart more than knowing you have a loyal friend, someone who will stand by you no matter what. A friend will defend you when you can't defend yourself. What an honor to know that this woman will stand up to tell the truth (or a lie, if necessary) to protect you, as illustrated by the loyalty shown by Jean to Rebecca.

Jean, now a corporate executive on the East Coast, fixed her friend Rebecca up with David — good looking, intelligent, seemingly sweet, and a member of a prominent family — who, as Rebecca later found out, was convinced that the women in his past each viewed him as the perfect catch that got away. Ten years after David and Rebecca ended their relationship, David and Jean ran into each other, and he alluded to the fond notion that Rebecca would likely never recover from losing him. Jean, a true friend, responded with, "Actually, David, I think Rebecca views you as one of a series of men that she dated for a period in her life and now questions why she did it." His eyes opened wide, and he was stunned into silence. Thank goodness for loyal girlfriends like this!

A loyal friend may stand up for us by standing up to us. Katherine, a writer and editor, acknowledged that as a child she was put down, not by other kids but by herself. She told us, "I thought I was being funny by putting myself down. I remember my friend Judy pulling me aside one time and saying, 'You know, it's not funny anymore.' And hearing it from her made me lighten up on constantly using myself as a butt of jokes."

Sometimes loyalty takes the form of supporting a friend as she sorts out what is best for her in another relationship. True girlfriends have an extraordinary ability to support us even as our situations evolve and change. Carey, a professional mediator, told us about her friend, "Ginna helped me get out of a painful marriage. She knew me and my husband, and she managed to be friendly to him, even though he was not a particularly nice person. She frequently stood up to him when he was angry with me, sometimes putting herself in the line of fire to protect me. Despite this she never suggested that I consider divorce. When the time came that I realized I could not stay in the marriage, Ginna was there for me every day, providing love and support. She even became my roommate, so I did not have to live alone. In large and small ways, she helped me through the most painful experience of my life."

Loyalty may require making a judgment call, as in the case of Jennifer, a nurse, who spoke up when she felt that her friend was not being treated right by the man she was dating. She told us, "My best friend was in love with this guy I knew treated her very poorly. How do you talk to someone about that? For a while I didn't say anything, but after a time I started telling her, 'That's not fair'; 'You know he's not doing things that he should be doing for you'; 'He's ignoring you'; and so on. She defended him, but she didn't get mad at me, because she knew that I was saying these things because I cared about her. Eventually they broke up, for which I was grateful. But then, to be loyal, I needed to support her while she grieved. I may not have liked the guy, but she had loved him for a long time. It's a hard balance, being angry at this guy but caring for her at the same time. It was hard also because then she was upset and sad."

Loyalty also shows itself in choosing to spend time with our girlfriends. Bethany, a recent recipient of a master's degree, told us, "I have a wonderful friend whom I only see when she travels to the West Coast on business. One time she flew in, and I told her I'd accommodate her business and social schedule. I knew she'd been invited out for a business dinner as well as to dinner with a male friend of hers. She told me, 'Absolutely not!' and she turned down these other invitations. She chose to spend time with me. She said, 'I want to come to your house for dinner and get into our robes and talk and talk.' To me, that feels like loyalty."

Many women have found that their girlfriends are there when no one else is, that the level of commitment remains constant no matter what else is going on in their lives. We may show loyalty to our friends by speaking up or merely showing up. Satiric author Fay Weldon offers her opinion of the value of her women friends in *Praxis:*

> We shelter children for a time; we live side by side with men; and that is all. We owe them nothing and are owed nothing. I think we owe our friends more, especially our female friends.[8]

Paying Attention

I always felt that the great high privilege, relief, and comfort of friendship was that one had to explain nothing.

—KATHERINE MANSFIELD

Deep friendships often result in knowing, frequently without asking, what the other feels and needs. Somehow our psyches become intertwined, and we know things about each other that we have no rational reason to know—no one told us, it's not written down anywhere. Of course, we may not always know all of the whys and wherefores, but we get the sense that something is wrong, and we find out the details.

Not only can women friends know what will comfort us, they also can know just what we need to hear about daily matters. As Elizabeth, a homemaker and mother of three from southern Missouri, writes, "Women are so busy being all things to all people, especially their families, that few men, children, and co-workers are aware of their needs. But, unlike most males I have come into contact with, close female friends notice everything. They compliment you when you've had your hair cut. They notice a new outfit. They acknowledge weight loss and ignore additional pounds. They are also intuitively aware when something's wrong yet won't press until you're ready to tell."

Even young girlfriends experience this attentive bond with each other, as seventeen-year-old Molly says of her friend, who is also named Molly, "You get more comfortable with each other. We're so close now it's like we read each other's minds. It's kind of weird."

Ellen, a West Coast psychologist, told us about the comfort she experienced when her friends attended to her during her mother's terminal illness. She said, "When my mother was dying, she lived in Georgia. My brother lives there, too; he was taking care of her, and I would fly to Georgia and stay with him while we cared for her. She was in intensive care for almost two months, and then a series of crises followed. I would fly to Georgia and then she would stabilize, so I'd go back home. There was a lot of back and forth. It was very stressful.

"Some of my friends, Janine and Maria and some others, put together this care package of all my favorite things at that time—books and tapes and foods and all kinds of things—and mailed it to my brother's house in Georgia for me. It was very lovely."

Colette, now in her late thirties, tells the story of a painful period in life when she found herself pregnant by an unsympathetic and uncaring man. "I'd told some of my friends that things were kind of rough, but I was *embarrassed* that I was in a relationship where I was in love like a teenager and it wasn't working. Here I thought it was the real thing and I wasn't being treated well. When I got pregnant I decided to get an abortion, but I didn't tell any friends about my situation, except for one, and that was not until right before I went in for the abortion. When I came home, there were flowers on the table and a note from her saying all the good stuff about me—how I had always been able to hear things and not be judgmental, and other things. Something like that went so far to help me in that period of my life."

Understanding what our friends need isn't magic. It comes from our taking the time to notice one another and respond to the needs we see or sometimes only intuit. Diane Sawyer sums it up succinctly, "I think the one thing that I have learned is that there is no substitute for paying attention."[9] Many women have been raised not to talk about their needs, not to complain if something is wrong, so friends who pay attention to our needs are especially precious. We all appreciate when someone notices we are hurting. This kind of attentiveness takes effort, and a real girlfriend makes the effort.

Honesty

The best mind-altering drug is truth.

—LILY TOMLIN

One may be my very good friend, and yet not of my opinion.

—MARGARET CAVENDISH (1664)

Being honest with one another is tough, especially for many women. But every woman needs a truth teller, and every relationship, in order to survive, requires that truth be told. We all know the sadness of friendships that fade because we can't bear to reveal our true feelings. It is easy yet ultimately painful to let someone drift away because of unresolved conflict. The relationship in which truth is told is one that can be trusted, and every woman we interviewed felt that friendships that go through troubled times are strengthened by the test.

A girlfriend is one who can admit if she is upset with you and you can admit the same to her. Many of us raised as "good girls" fear conflict in a relationship because we do not realize that a real friendship can sustain conflict. Marilyn tells about Penny, a close girlfriend she's had for ten years. She said, "Penny came from a family where the expression of anger was not allowed. So, at the beginning of our relationship, I knew she was angry because she'd start acting weird, sort of withdrawn, not her usually enthusiastic self. I'd ask her if she was upset about something, and in a rush of emotion Penny would finally tell the truth about how she was feeling. After we sorted it all out, Penny would often tear up and say how surprised she was that our relationship could withstand anger. I told her that anger didn't scare me, but I was afraid of what would happen if she continued to hold in her feelings. As the years have gone by, Penny is much better about coming out with it right away, telling me she didn't like something I did or said. It gives me much more confidence in the future of our relationship now that she's willing to admit her feelings."

Some people may be afraid that they will lose a friend if they express a negative opinion or feeling. Stories such as the one told by Faye, now in her fifties, about her friend Eleanor, illustrate that friends can even argue without losing the friendship. "In twenty-five years of friendship, we have had two fights—one about four months ago. And it was a lulu. We fought while talking on the telephone, and it was over an oven, of all things. We both owned the same horrendous piece of garbage that I unfortunately steered her to buy because I read about it. As it turns out, the fight wasn't about an oven at all but about the different ways we navigate life. We both had very personal ideas about what the outcome of this argument should be. We were isolated from each other because of our locked-in agendas. We were able to figure it out the following day."

Differences as individuals will invariably lead to differences of opinions between them, and may foster serious arguments, such as the one between Faye and Eleanor. We can defuse those arguments when we realize that differences of opinions are rarely about right or wrong—they are reflections of who we are as individuals. Friendships that mature beyond a bond of commonality to make room for differences are those strong enough to withstand the tests of time and change. And they give us what we all so desperately need—a safe, complete acceptance of who we are.

Good friends can also withstand our losing control of ourselves from time to time. Faye continued, "We love each other so much that we are almost over a fight the next day. One fight I hung up on her. She never loses control; I do. I was livid. I screamed at her and hung up on her. That's the first time in twenty-five years." We asked her if she felt the friendship would end in one of those fights, and Faye responded, "Never, never, never, never, never. We're too important to each other."

Helen, a forty-six-year-old publicist, appreciates when someone has been honest with her, even though it was painful at the time: "I was involved in a five-year relationship with a very charismatic person who had a substance abuse problem. My father is an alcoholic, and I tended to be attracted to men who had that potential. This man was a tall, brooding poet, and he drove a cab and took cocaine to keep awake and to write late at night, and of course nothing ever got edited or published. The relationship was bad, and I was getting more and more involved in his world. One night this man and I had a party and about halfway through the party one of my friends—not even a very close girlfriend—said she wanted to talk to me. We went into another room and shut the door, and she just looked me right in the eye and said, 'This is scary; he has a problem and you have a problem and I really want you to deal with this.' It was like she had thrown cold water in my face in the middle of our party. I was shocked and angry and just returned to the party.

"The next day we talked again, and about a year and a half later violence occurred in the relationship, and she was the one I went to at midnight. I ended up staying at her house, and then I lived with her for a while. About a year and a half later I had to talk to her equally honestly about something that I saw her doing that I felt was unhealthy— an issue that I felt she was skirting around. She didn't like it either, but she had opened that honesty door between us, and I think that took a lot of courage."

When a friendship is really strong, one friend may voice thoughts, feelings, or perspectives which the other may not be able to voice herself. It does, however, have its risks if the friend isn't receptive to what is being said. Donna, a forty-year-old marketing consultant, has had to face this risk: "I have a really good friend who has some emotional issues, and they get in the way of her really seeing her problems. So she keeps repeating the same thing over and over and over and making the same mistakes and clinging to the same fears. And our friendship will never progress past a certain point as a result of that. It takes courage and the ability to accept what other people are saying in order to have a real, full friendship." Friendship is limited when we are not honest with our friends, but also, as Donna's relationship indicates, when we don't allow a friend to tell us what she perceives as the truth. We may not ultimately agree, but if our friend is trying to tell us something, perhaps we need to take some time to listen.

Stephanie Salter, columnist for the *San Francisco Examiner*, values her lifelong friends because "when you're telling them something, if it is bullshit, you can hear it in your own ears, because you know they know. They can keep you honest, the way I think visiting home again can keep you honest when you get the idea that who you are is totally independent of who you were." Honesty with a friend means speaking the truth with the intent of doing the best thing for the friend. However, honesty is not always about soul-searching issues. For instance, Susan told her close friend not to buy a certain dress, as she looked like Kermit the Frog. One of the author's friends says her glasses make her look like Tweety Bird. Girlfriends can tell you if your hair color is bad or if your boyfriend lied to you. The interesting thing is, so can your worst enemy. The difference is that your girlfriend does not relish it, and you just know that in your bones.

The Bonds of Humor

*One can never speak enough of the virtues, the dangers,
the power of shared laughter.*

—FRANÇOISE SAGAN

Many beautiful friendships arise and grow from a shared
sense of humor. As Allison, a flower warehouse manager,
avows, "My girlfriends and I have one rule: we can never
go out with a guy or be friends with anyone who can't make
us laugh. It's a good rule to follow."

Vanessa, sixteen, told us that Melissa has become one of
her closest friendships due to a shared sense of humor. "We
became close friends on a camping trip with our church
youth group. The first time we ever laughed together, just
the two of us, it lasted for half an hour until we were gasp-
ing helplessly for air and clutching our aching stomachs.
We were lying on the beach in California, giggling so force-
fully we had sore muscles the next day. One of the things
that amazes me about Melissa is that we both have the
same twisted sense of humor. Many times we have been at
a movie or watching a television show, and something that
is not supposed to be humorous will send us rolling down
the aisles. I have felt very alone without her, chortling at
something and finding people staring. Together we are the
essence of silliness. We sing silly songs, give huge bear
hugs, make silly noises, and play silly games. This part of

our friendship has saved us both from scary or sad situations. We have learned to deal with the aspects of our friendship that are in need of work or healing by balancing the seriousness with simple happiness."

Lest we believe that silliness is reserved for the young, Fern, a sixty-two-year-old Midwesterner, tells this story: "My friends Connie, Sandy, and I, when we were all in our thirties and forties, were together on a vacation in Florida. Connie had been ill and we were all tired of the cold winter weather, so we decided to spend a few days in the sun. Connie had always been very reserved and discreet, with a Grace Kelly-like sophistication. At dinner one night, we started talking about the kinds of things we do for our husbands, whom we loved but who nevertheless could be exasperating. Suddenly a wry smile crept across Connie's face, as she told us in great detail how her husband required twelve chocolate chips in each of his chocolate chip cookies and how she actually counted them out for each cookie. The image of that devotion started all of us chortling. Then she went on to describe how she patiently (or not so patiently) reironed all his starched shirts from the laundry, because he didn't like the creases that the laundry left in his shirts. She revealed that she had a mantra while performing this redundant chore: 'I love my husband, I love my husband, I love my husband' (through clenched teeth). We were roaring, laughing so hard we couldn't eat. Everyone at the restaurant was staring, although I could tell all of the women wanted to be at our table. We had such a wonderful evening, and it provided a base for the layers of fun and enjoyment of the entire vacation."

Sometimes laughter is the only thing left to do and, quite possibly, the only thing that helps. Author Sue Monk Kidd tells this story of when her friend Betty was diagnosed with cancer: "Betty was in the hospital, having been told she would probably not live out the year. Everything was so serious and grim and heavy. She was lying there in bed with tubes coming out of nearly every available orifice, and I smiled at her and said, 'You know, you've got really bad hair.' Her hair was genuinely terrible. I mean, she hadn't washed it for weeks through all those surgeries. 'I know, it's horrible,' said Betty. I asked her if she wanted me to wash it. We weren't supposed to do that, of course. She was sick and there were those tubes and half a million stitches from surgery. But bad hair is bad hair. Besides that, we had never been known for being sensible.

"Individually we might have been ordinary women, but together we became Bette Midler thumbing our noses at prudence. 'Yeah,' she said, 'wash it. Wash the stuff.' So I helped her get up, practically carried her and her entourage of tubes to the bathroom, and sat her on the side of the tub. Then I got the sprayer and began washing her hair. But the hose was unruly and she was soaked — her nightgown, everything. We stared at each other a minute, then burst into laughter.

"We laughed and laughed and laughed until the laughter took on a life of its own. We couldn't stop. And there was really something thrilling about that — for her to be laughing like this in the midst of all this angst and pain. I mean, my friend was facing death, and she was laughing her head off. She was living in the moment, finding whatever joy there was and wringing it out. That was ten years ago, and she is still going. Still laughing, still thumbing her nose at prudence."

Shared laughter offers us pleasure during the fun times and a resilient strength during distress. Sometimes life just seems too ridiculous and unexplainable. Laughing by yourself in these times seems somehow bitter and mirthless, but, as Sue and Betty discovered, laughter shared with a friend feels sweet and healing.

Independence

Constant togetherness is fine — but only for Siamese twins.

—VICTORIA BILLINGS

While our lives seem inexplicably tied up in the lives of our friends, these bonds do not weigh heavily. Many women express appreciation for the freedom and independence they find in their relationships with women friends. Cynthia told us, "The thing I appreciate the most is that we don't have to hang out all the time or be on the phone with each other for hours on end. We are all pretty independent.

I don't care for relationships that are too dependent on each other."

This appreciation seems to grow as we get older and our time and attention become absorbed by an ever-expanding number of matters. When Elizabeth, a mother of three in her midthirties, was asked what she most valued about her relationships with her close women friends she exclaimed, "Freedom! A friendship that has no pressure, no demands and no job description! We don't want to be stifled with unnecessary lunch commitments, unending and time-wasting telephone calls. Our time is important, and my friends know that."

Holly, a mother of two from New Jersey, also appreciates this freedom. "I have made quite a few close friends. We share a lot. We all have kids, some grown and out of the house, others just starting families. We have our own busy families. We aren't looking for that possessive best friend of our youth. That frees us to really share and get support for the difficult or confusing aspects of our lives."

The freedom of which these women speak allows friends to follow their sometimes very different paths and yet continue to celebrate their friendship throughout their lives. Karen, an editor and author, told us about growing up with Beth and having their relationship develop in an easy, natural way. "Beth was better than I at climbing and crossing streams on narrow logs and other things that required physical agility and daring. I was better than she at school; Beth was dyslexic. I don't remember ever feeling jealous of her talents or superior because of mine: I don't remember feeling competitive, just complementary.

"Beth didn't go to college because she couldn't read well; she became one of the first professional woman firefighters in our county—she was a martial arts phenomenon even though she was a petite, sexy little thing with a trained contralto voice. She married a fireman, and I finished college. When I married, Beth was my matron of honor, vamping the photographer until he blushed. But I moved to Colorado, and we lost touch.

"Ten years later, I had a book published, and word came back to me that Beth would really like a copy. I was amazed, since I knew Beth rarely read anything, and I thought perhaps ten years had put our friendship in the distant past for her. But I took the opportunity to inscribe a copy of my book with some words I would never have thought to voice but had always wanted to say. I told her, and meant it, that I would never have survived my childhood without her and would always be more grateful to her for her love that she would ever know.

"Beth wants me to write the story of her life one day. It's a great plot, and I bet it would sell. She tells a good story, but she can hardly write. But I can write, and someday I hope to write a tribute to my best buddy."

Olive Dickason and Carlotta Blue, well-known Canadian writers, look back on fifty-six years of friendship that provided both support and independence. During World War II, these aspiring, young writers competed for "men's jobs" in the writing fields, and these ground-breaking women celebrated their first by-lines together. Carlotta said their long friendship has endured throughout. "We rarely talk on the phone unless we have something specific to say. We assume we're both going on about the business of our lives. We both know we can cry on each other's shoulders if we need to." Olive agreed, "Sometimes long periods of time can go by, but we never lose touch. There was no great urgency about it. It just happened."[10]

Whether the cord of independence stretches to allow for emotional space or spans years of separation, it is strong and unbreakable, eventually drawing us back to one another. And when we return to share the stories of our adventures, we have the opportunity to celebrate our differences and take pride in our loose-fitting, but lasting bonds.

Get a Grip!

Surely we ought to prize those friends on whose principles and opinions we may constantly rely —of whom we may say in all emergencies, "I know what they would think."

—HANNAH FARNHAM LEE (1844)

Sometimes we need a friend to give us a kick start to break out of a bad habit or a negative way of looking at ourselves. When we need to get a grip, a true girlfriend will offer helpful suggestions and, if ever necessary, she will take charge.

Annette, a management consultant, says that the important thing is that the friend's impatience be wrapped in kindness and generosity, as illustrated by the following story told by one of the authors.

Tamara tells this story: "One night in college, I was studying for a calculus exam far into the night. Although I had enjoyed the class and working out the problems, all of a sudden I froze and could not absorb anything. My heart was racing. I went back to my dorm room and began fairly bubbling hysteria to my roommate. I was pacing and literally wringing my hands, while she sat and watched me over her glasses and book.

"'*Tamara,*' her voice cut through, 'there is a bottle of Scotch in the closet left over from our last party. I want you to pick up that glass, go over to the closet, pour yourself a shot, and drink it.' I just stared at her; was she crazy? I was studying for a *calculus* exam, for heaven's sake. 'Just do it,' she commanded. And I did it. As the Scotch burned its way down my throat, it seemed to cut a hole right through the panic. I just looked at her dumbly and said, 'Thanks, I needed that.' I felt like I was in the old aftershave ad. And, happy ending, I got an A on the exam. Thank God for Betsy."

Sally, a first-time author, described how she went through a meltdown at the thought of seeing her name in print. She told us, "I was just wigging out. I was completely convinced that I had written something totally stupid and everyone who saw it was going to think I was the most ridiculous person on earth. I would lie awake at night and stare at the ceiling and worry, night after night after night. Finally my girlfriend said, 'You know this isn't real, don't you?' She validated my feelings but didn't let me get away with my weird thinking. As soon as I recognized my feelings for what they were, the whole thing sort of went away. I am so grateful to her for that."

At other times, we may need someone to support us in our decisions and help us to clarify our thinking if we get muddled in the process of living them out. If it weren't for our friends to observe, comment, and encourage, would any of us make changes in our lives? Laurie, a graduate student, talks about her experience: "I am making a transition from a career as an investment banker, which was not my life's calling, to a career as a psychologist, which I believe is my life's calling. In gaining strength and courage enough to make the transition, I am forever indebted to Lisa, who knew me and believed in me more than I knew and believed in myself."

Sometimes love is soft and sweet, nice and nurturing. But often the love that is needed is strong, confrontive, and clear. Sentimentality is tossed aside for the penetrating vision of someone who knows us well and cares enough to take us on. When we are confused, we can rely on these girlfriends to point the way to clarity and maybe even to give us the necessary boot to get started.

Being There

I can trust my friends. These people force me to examine,
encourage me to grow.

—CHER

Many women say they appreciate their friends "being there" for them. We believe that "being there" requires the ability to empathize. One definition of empathy is "the capacity to participate in another's feelings or ideas."[11] The knowledge that the other person is accompanying us, is able to appreciate our feelings or ideas without necessarily agreeing with us, is powerful.

"Being there" also includes giving encouragement. We all need support, especially when we are exploring new talents or attempting a life change. Our friends can come to know our danger spots—the places where the bridge goes out most often—and help shore us up, give that extra oomph, the push, the clear-eyed reminder that we are doing the right thing. They also remind us when we are sliding from the path that is good for us or forgetting our value.

Anne, a forty-year-old entrepreneur, told us about her experience in starting up a new business with Chris, who is turning into a friend as well as a business associate. She said, "We're out on a limb together with the chain saw running, but the relationship is more than that. As we go down this road, we're learning about each other—what we're frightened of, what we're good at, what we don't like to do.

We're mutually supporting and helping and pushing each other. One will say, 'I can't do that yet,' and the other will say, 'Oh, yes you can!' and so on. It's getting us through some very stressful and exciting days."

We believe that sometimes each of us is blessed with real empathy. Sometimes we can keep so still in our own mind, not focusing on our own agenda for our friend, that we can snatch a sense of what she truly needs. Sandra's friend, who was struggling to break out of an abusive relationship, probably kept coming to Sandra for empathy and encouragement because Sandra continued to recognize and acknowledge the steps that she was taking to get out of the situation, no matter how subtle. When we have that intuitive connection with a friend, we know if she needs us to say, "You need to be doing more," and when you need to say, "That's really great that you took that little step."

Sue told us about how she encouraged her friend Betty after Betty was diagnosed with terminal cancer. Sue said, "I remember sitting in the hospital room holding hands while she said, 'I will not die!' with me repeating back to her, 'You will not die.' She is still alive, ten years later, but we went through years of not knowing whether she would live or not.

"A lot of things that we feel helped save Betty's life were things that we did together, unconventional things that we'd never done before. Betty felt she'd boxed herself into a very tight, conventional way of life and had not allowed her female self any freedom. It was true of me too. So we would go out to the woods and dance or dress up in wild hats with ostrich feathers in them and wear outlandish outfits. We'd pretend to be the Bette Midler character in the movie *Beaches*, that outlandish, free, feisty broad that Betty needed and I needed, too. We would dare one another; that was part of our relationship. It was outlandish and wild and wonderful, and we laughed and laughed. It was really important."

Mary, in her midthirties, tells of her friend Susan, who encourages and inspires her, even when Susan is the one suffering. Mary told us, "When Susan's child Aaron was born in 1990 with an open laceration to his brain, she and her husband were informed that he had a chromosome disorder, Trisomy-13, with a terminal prognosis. Aaron should already be dead according to all the experts. Although his survival is miraculous, Aaron's needs are constant, and the emotional and financial drain on my friend concerns me the most. Susan has reached great heights of courage. She is a true hero. When her mind is sore, heart empty, and her body exhausted, I can hear her soul whispering clearly, 'Keep living, loving, and laughing.' All I can do is offer Susan a hug, an ear, and time; I am her girlfriend.

"Even with this burden on her shoulders, she has taken time to give me another gift: she has taught me not to fear the handicapped. I spent most of my life running from the handicapped, afraid to touch them because, 'if I touch you, I will be like you.' I could not appreciate minds that were of lesser intelligence than mine. As Susan learned about her gifted child, so did I. She would share books and literature and invite me to support group seminars, and slowly my fears were healed."

"Being there" includes both empathy, the willingness to put ourselves in our friend's place, and the offering of encouragement when our friend's supply of faith is low. Sometimes, as in Mary and Susan and Betty and Sue's cases, the encouragement we give to our friends is reciprocated simultaneously. Mary gave support to Susan while Susan encouraged Mary to accept a handicapped child. Sue shared her faith, and Betty helped assuage Sue's fear of Betty's death. Shared encouragement and empathy can propel us further than we would ever be able to go if left on our own. Sometimes there is no greater gift we can give each other than simply "being there."

Soul Connection

There are these huge thunderstorms,
and we sit out on the porch in rocking chairs
with coffee and talk, and comes the dawn.

—ROBIN WILLIAMS

Some friendships are so strong, they become part of us; they become visceral. "We're in each other's blood," says Gina of her friend Faith and herself; they have been friends for thirty-five years since they grew up in southern Wisconsin. Rachel Anne, a retired teacher in her early seventies, reveals the formula for maintaining a lifelong friendship with her friend Joyce even though she has moved and changed over the years of her life: "There's no real secret about it; it's just that our lives crossed in a very meaningful way. Our mothers were friends, we had a lot of basic common experiences, we graduated from the same high school, and so forth. She still lives on the shores of Lake Okoboji, where I grew up and where my great-grandfather homesteaded. Generation after generation of contacts means that, even when time and space have intervened, there's still a lot of basic shared fabric."

Common experience can cultivate a soul connection between women. Susan, book industry executive and mother of two daughters, told us about Jeanette, also a single mother who lives about eight blocks from her home. Susan said, "Jeanette is about the same age that I am, coincidentally has two daughters, and our girls are friends with each other. We are both divorced, and we've had a lot of shared experiences. She has listened to me when I've ranted and raved about things, and I've listened to her do the same. We carpool, the girls take swimming lessons together, and we do various other activities together. We're always available to each other. We also have nearly the same birthday—hers is May 21 and mine is May 22."

Sometimes you become so connected with a friend that other people mistake you for each other. Perhaps they have merely linked your names in their minds because you are with your friend frequently, or perhaps there is a more ephemeral reason: when two people share an intuitive link, other people unconsciously pick up that link. Anne, an early childhood educator, recalled such an incident involving her friend: "I was walking down the street one day and ran into a man who was a mutual friend of mine and of a college friend. We said hello, and he exclaimed, 'Oh, Shirley, you've had your baby!' I walked on, completely bewildered, for about a block, until I realized he was talking about my college friend Shirley!"

Sometimes we become so identified with a friend that we begin noticing we have both clicked into the same mental track. Martha, a homemaker from Pennsylvania, described "tracking" her friend: "In high school, when we were closest, we were so in sync that we didn't need to verbalize our thoughts some of the time. We frequently showed up wearing the same or similar outfits." Helen, a songwriter, has had the same experience with her friend Marianne: "We think so much alike sometimes that once we bought identical sequined blouses without the other's knowledge."

And then there are the physical connections, which are sometimes eerie and always unexplainable. For instance, when Marianne broke her right ankle and Helen broke her left ankle just one week apart, their husbands thought they'd taken this female bonding a bit far. And Tamara, one of the authors, tells this story: "After years of talking, planning, and dreaming, my friend Laura and I both left our careers as lawyers in large, corporate law firms. Both of us were pursuing our dreams; she wanted to be a theatrical producer, and I had decided to get involved in publishing. She was producing her very first play on Broadway, and it was opening to much critical acclaim. I was invited to the opening of the play and was so proud of my friend; to have accomplished so much in so little time underscored the hard-won belief that one did not have to be afraid of pursuing one's dreams. I was thrilled to see her there, in the middle of all that attention, but I felt somewhat puzzled (and impressed) that she seemed so calm and relaxed. I became completely absorbed in the play, but as the closing scene began, I felt an overwhelming sense of nausea. I missed the last scene as I rushed to the bathroom to throw up! When I told her about my misfortune, she understood immediately and thanked me for getting sick for her. We both knew exactly what had happened."

Darlene, a psychotherapist, describes what she calls the "soul connection" she has with a couple of women friends. She explains, "Our bond defies time. Our paths may not cross for the longest time, but when we get back together it's like no time has passed. We have enough common interests and a willingness to be real—to get to that level where you really share what's going on in your mind and your heart. I guess the back-and-forthness of it is really valuable, especially to me, since as a therapist I spend so much time listening. It's so nice to be able to blab and have somebody listen to me for a change. But its really the intensity and completeness within a moment that gives us such a soul connection."

Some women refer to a male lover as a soulmate, and yet sharing that kind of bond with another woman brings its own unique pleasures. There are certain things that never have to be explained to a female friend—the essence of being a woman at this point in history. A soul connection can develop from different points of commonality. Rachel Anne and Joyce and Susan and Jeanette built their soul connections on common life experiences. Helen and Marianne shared an almost psychic connection while Tamara and Laura bonded through launching major life transitions at the same time. This common knowledge, on an experiential, intuitive, or even psychic level, can bond us powerfully and forever.

Friend as Counselor

What do we live for, if it is not to make life less difficult for each other?

—GEORGE ELIOT (c. 1850)

One aspect of the age in which we live is that many people see psychotherapists or counselors. People who in past decades would have gone to visit their minister or rabbi or consulted an older, wiser member of the family now may visit a counselor to work through their problems. One woman commented that therapy could be considered "paid friendship" and that if we had a good circle of caring friends who were good listeners, we'd have less need to rely on professional therapists.

Of course, friendship will not solve all psychological ills. But for the day-to-day counseling, the reciprocal listening without judgment, our friends can be invaluable. Janice, thirty-seven, describes her experience: "We can listen to each other in a nonjudgmental way. The other day, my friend, who is working in her husband's family business, called me and said she had yelled at her brother-in-law while at work. She had been loud, and she felt awful about how she had handled herself. Her husband was upset with her, too. We have shared many ugly stories about ourselves, and usually we just need to have someone hear about whatever happened. This time, however, I offered some advice. My friend called her brother-in-law, and they had a very

104

productive conversation. That's just one of many examples of how we help each other."

Friends often provide a listening ear over the phone. Something about the telephone allows us to fully unburden ourselves. It is the modern confessional, the dark booth in which we are alone and yet not alone, where we can spill out the things about which we are most ashamed. By not having to face a friend, we can get the dark secrets or unexplainable feelings out. Seventeen-year-old Molly told us, "When I'm talking about a difficult subject, it's just easier not to actually be there looking at her. I can't really see her reaction, so I can just tell my story without being inhibited. I'm much more relaxed and able to talk openly when I'm on the phone."

One of the most valuable characteristics of a counselor is confidentiality. Contrary to the myths of popular culture whereby women are supposedly unable to keep a secret, we found that confidentiality is an attribute most appreciated and respected by women. Over and over again, women responded to the question of what characteristics they valued most about a friendship with "the ability to keep a secret." As Patty, a homemaker from southern Illinois, says, "We all know that we have things that happen in our lives that we don't want everyone to know but that we need to vent or talk about. I can't stress enough how I value people keeping a secret."

Sometimes we tell a friend our secret because we need to try it out on someone and learn if we can still be accepted by her. Janet, a sales manager, says the closeness of a friendship is defined by the ability to "know the dark side of someone and love her anyway." Rene, a resource teacher, explains, "I can express my dreams, fantasies, or fears without anxiety because I know they will remain in confidence and I won't be considered crazy. I can pick up the phone and call my friend Eleanor, even if it's just to say, 'I just needed to say this out loud to someone.' I know she will listen with love and acceptance, giving me her perspective if I ask for it or just lending a listening ear."

Perhaps KC, a dancer and choreographer, said it most vividly: "One of the things I most admire about my friendship with Holly is that I can say even the ugly stuff about myself to her. I'm realizing how important that is. I can say anything. I feel very free and very open and unjudged by Holly in this friendship, and that's a tremendous thing for me. I think we often spend a lot of time feeling guilty about the negative things that we think inside, but they're part of us and they're also passing through us. I value being able to express that to somebody without her saying, 'Oh, yuck, you think that, or you feel that?' That's very valuable."

No one knows why feeling accepted, completely, faults and all, is so powerfully healing. We just know that we are transformed when someone else listens to us, taking in our experience. For the listening ear, the assurance of confidentiality, and the well-placed word of advice, we thank our women friends.

Surviving the Rough Spots

*Disagreements have been part of our relationship —
along with forgiveness — as we are totally different
personalities and love always remains.*

—CLAUDETTE RENNER

*Trouble is a sieve through which we sift our acquaintances.
Those too big to pass through are our friends.*

—ARLENE FRANCIS

Rocky periods in friendships tend to be like broken bones — painful and debilitating but, once healed, making the relationship stronger than ever. Beth has been friends with Melanie since they were fourteen (they are now forty something). In that friendship, they shared their teen years and experienced their first boyfriends, school exams, and family issues. They went through a difficult phase when they were both in their early twenties. "We were far from home, and she was dating my brother — jealousy perhaps? I was unhappy — an awful boring job, no social life in a new city — we just had nothing in common to discuss! We didn't address the distance between us but let things drift. A big mistake, but we were both younger. I moved away again.

"When we got in contact again, things improved. Since then we have discussed this situation and cleared subsequent issues in a far better, open, and more mature way. Now that we are older, we have decided that the best way to confront problems is to talk them out openly. Now we are as close as ever."

Making the leap—allowing yourself to be vulnerable and speak out when you notice something feels wrong in the friendship—requires courage and commitment. Judy, who had been suffering with a bout of cancer, and her friend Mona, who had been dealing with family illness, found themselves drawing apart by being too protective of each other. Judy described an important exchange they had: "We'd been very real and close with each other, and at some point I noticed that we hadn't had much time together. I knew that she'd been in a very stressful place in her life. So I began telling myself, 'Well, we love each other, and it's just because of circumstances on both sides that we can't get together.' (Because of my low white blood cell count, I sometimes couldn't see her if somebody in her family was sick.) At some point I spoke to her about this, and she said that she thought I had a full plate and she couldn't ask anything of me. I said to her, 'We have both slightly, unconsciously backed off because we're both so aware of the other person's full plate.' We both knew that there are circumstances where maybe somebody couldn't be there at a given time, but I wanted us to be open, get that passage-way open again, because the backing off is so subtle. Particularly, what I've been dealing with is people backing away from me because they're afraid of what's happening to me. So to find that in this best of all possible friendships was surprising. Being able to pinpoint the issue has brought it to our full awareness and made it easier for us both."

Judy continued, "We may or may not be able to get together at a given moment. Something happens like today"—Mona was unable to come to the interview because of illness—"and I could hear the regret in her voice when she said, 'I'm just so disappointed for me, and I hate doing this to you.' And yet, something has been cleared in our passage so that we don't worry about asking something of each other. The feeling of an open passage is very, very significant. To me, it's a foundation."

Sometimes abject and shared misery can break down a wall that forms between friends. We interviewed two women, Cynthia and Maggie, both in their late thirties, who worked together and who had been having some problems communicating for a while. Cynthia described how a mutually miserable social event ended up breaking down the barrier that had arisen between them.

Cynthia began: "Maggie and I had been invited to a wedding of a co-worker. Both of the men we had been involved with were there. I had just broken up with the man I was involved with because he was a faithless infidel, and Maggie's relationship was unraveling as well. The wedding was being held in a distant suburb of Chicago, where we lived, and we made the critical mistake of getting a ride from someone else to the wedding and reception. So we were stuck until our ride decided he was ready to leave.

"During the entire reception, the man who had been involved with Maggie was making passes at another woman, and the man who I had just broken up with picked a bridesmaid to flirt with, dance with, and generally illustrate what a jerk he was. All of our work companions were there, and we had to pretend that everything was fine and we were having a good time. It was just horrifying, and we were stranded. For relief, we would go off occasionally and smoke a cigarette (we didn't smoke). Finally, after a decent amount of time, we turned to each other and said, 'We must get out of here.' We literally stood in the parking lot waiting for someone to leave so we could ask for a ride. By the time we got back to the city, we were so exhausted from the charade and so relieved to be out of there that all our defenses were down. Everything that had been bothering both of us about our relationship came tumbling out. We cried and told the truth, and it was an important transition point in the friendship."

Sharing misery is not the only way to make it possible to talk through a rough spot in a friendship. However, if the relationship seems difficult, sometimes it helps to look at all that you and your friend have in common and all that you stand to lose without each other. Maggie and Cynthia were grateful for each other's presence that night, and their gratitude overcame their barrier. The ability of these women friends to talk over their differences, or as Judy analogizes, to keep the passages open, has helped these women get through the rough spots. It may take years to approach each other, like Beth and Melanie, but it is never too late to try to clear up a sore spot in a relationship.

Refreshment

Those who are unhappy have no need for anything in
this world but people capable of giving them attention.

—SIMONE WEIL

We go to our friends for nourishment, both figuratively and literally. Kristine, a house cleaner from Minnesota, says that what she most appreciates about getting together with her friends is that she can "come with all baggage attached and leave feeling refreshed and energized." Patricia describes time spent with her friends as "time out, total relaxation."

What kind of magic happens with our friends? A simple magic: a shared cup of tea, a walk on the beach or around the block, just connection. Replenishment can be an easy thing. Arlene, an author, lyrically describes the pleasures of spending time with her friend Margit, a yoga teacher, where they both come away mutually replenished, spiritually and physically: "The morning is dreary. Rain clouds gathering. I rested fitfully last night, and so I feel drained of energy, head foggy, bones achy. She's as cheery as ever, having a cup of tea. Later we start to make lunch. The rhythms are natural. She starts the preparations while I read something she has written. I take over the seasoning of the soup and the final touches while she reads something I have written. The combination of our two efforts makes our writing, as well as our soup, more interesting to both of us than our usual individual attempts. And we both cherish each other's viewpoints and suggestions in the lunch conversation. We also both know when we are full—satisfied, nourished, heart, stomach, soul, body—and it's time to say good-bye and take the refreshed energy back into our own work."

One woman explained how a most thoughtful friend helped her through several difficult times in her life "by merely insisting that I join various dinner parties at her house. When my heart had been trampled in the dust by a love affair gone awry, when I was feeling so trapped in my career I thought I would explode, I had a tendency to hole up in my apartment, cry, and eat junk food. The problems would seem to get bigger and bigger as I sat there alone.

"She would call at the right time, and I would pour out my problems. After listening carefully and calmly, she, an inveterate hostess, would say, 'I think you should come over to my house for dinner tonight.' I would wail in return, 'I'm not hungry, I've been eating junk food all day, and I'm in too bad a mood.' She would insist that I needed to be around some people and then would insist that I come over early to 'help her cook.' Helping her cook, I would realize, often meant that I would stir the risotto while she plied me with sherry and made me realize that my problems would not destroy me and the world was not falling apart after all."

Replenishment can also result in a change of life's focus. Carmen, one of the authors and a massage and body worker in southern California, credits her friend Bobette with introducing her to the benefits of massage over a decade ago. She said, "I was what I now call 'a walking head.' I was totally out of touch with my body. Then Bobette talked me into going to a hot springs one summer and trying out a mud bath and massage. I would never have gone if she hadn't put the trip all together. There we were, floating in mud, sipping our water from straws, and having the time of our lives. And then I had my first massage. Whoooosh! What a surprise to find I had a body! That day marked a new era for me personally and professionally, and all because Bobette insisted I try something new!"

Often we can view relaxing or taking care of ourselves as a luxury. But the refreshment of body and spirit, available through our connections with other women, can add years to our lives, replenish us after a dry period, or even start a new phase of life. Our friends can rejuvenate us by just letting us be, or they may drag our tired spirits and bodies, frequently protesting, to a place (physical or mental) where we will be renewed.

Strength

À coeur vaillant rien d'impossible.
Nothing is impossible to a valiant heart.

—JEANNE D'ALBRET (Motto adopted by her son Henry IV, c. 1550)

Almost everyone we talked to said she loved *Little Women* as a girl, either in the book or the movie form. Anna Quindlen, in her *New York Times* column of April 29, 1990, said she had done an informal survey among the men and women she knew, and not one of the men knew who Jo March was: "One guessed that Jo March was a second baseman for the Baltimore Orioles."[12] On the other hand, every woman she talked to answered the question correctly. Why do so many of us identify with Jo? Anna Quindlen's theory is that "Jo is the smart one, and that is why she left an indelible mark. She showed that there was more to life than spinning skeins into gold and marrying a prince." However, there is another aspect of Jo which impresses us—she is also the strong one.

At certain times in our lives, we need to rely on the strength of our friends. Sue Bender, author of *Plain and Simple,* credits her friendship with Mitzi McClosky, a therapist, with giving her the courage to give birth to her book. "Without Mitzi and our conversations, I never could have done it. We met informally once a week, a meeting that for me became a sacred ritual. She is my beloved friend, somebody who tells the truth and reflects back on things."

Sue told us she was very grateful for Mitzi's support, but for some time felt uncertain as to what she was giving in exchange. Several years later, their roles reversed, and their relationship now illustrates the miracle of friendship—how we trade roles and exchange gifts. Mitzi described herself as becoming "obsessed" with the problems and issues connected with caregiving for elderly parents, and began keeping notes and writing thoughts on the subject on the backs of envelopes and in her journal. Sue then began encouraging her to put all her jottings into a book. As Mitzi describes, "Thanks to Sue's prompting, I arranged the material and began to type it up. I now have a complete manuscript—*Mollie's Golden Years*. Sue's and my roles have reversed. Sue has read what I've written and I think she wrote the most eloquent criticism—thoughtful and honest—that I have ever seen. Receiving help had always been difficult for me. Sue taught me how to accept a gift with generosity of spirit. From her I learned that receiving can be a gift to the giver."

Women also gain strength in groups; packs of women can get more accomplished than one woman alone. And working in a group can give us the courage and momentum to step in where we wouldn't necessarily have done so alone. Martha, now a homemaker in Pennsylvania, found that she and her friends could accomplish a great deal together: "When I worked as an administrative manager for a large company, three other women in approximately equivalent positions and I got in the habit of meeting for coffee breaks and sometimes lunch together. We shared our frustrations and sympathized with one another.

"Just before Christmas one woman found out that one of her employees had been evicted and would be living in her car with her son and pregnant daughter. We organized a fund-raising drive and in three days raised first, last, and deposit payments. We celebrated by having dinner together and drinking Pink Ladies. We became 'The Pink Ladies,' and each had a club name (Scarlett, Wonder Woman, BonBon, and Miss Feathers). We had regular dinners after that, and ten years later, all working for different companies—and me having moved away—we still stay in touch and meet when we can."

Women who have banded together not only get a lot done; they also gather a surprising amount of power. Sandra Martz, founder of Papier-Mache Press and editor of *When I Am an Old Woman I Shall Wear Purple*, told us this story of a group of friends that formed over twenty years ago: "In the early seventies, I was working for a large corporation in a clerical job. This was about the time that the women's movement reared its head. The corporation I worked for was a government contractor and under the review of the Equal Employment Opportunity Commission, who audited companies on issues of equality in the workplace. At the same time, there was a lot of grass roots organizing on the part of women in the company. Some of these women began to get involved in company-sponsored affirmative action programs and special committees. There was a particular committee composed of all women, of which I eventually became a member, that acted as an advisory group to top management. After a while, we began to feel that management was using the group to placate the EEOC officers when they would come in. We felt that management was pointing to us and saying, 'We're really doing great. Look how we've got this group of women who identifies women's concerns and we respond to their needs.' In reality many of the big issues that the group identified, such as child care and putting women into management roles, were never addressed.

"Our feelings culminated in what we perceived as a very radical act, which was to disband the committee. We all got together in someone's living room and signed a letter of resignation, saying, 'We're not going to be your vehicle anymore,' and presented it to the head of the company. It was really exciting and felt very radical. This act of defiance cemented the bonds that had already started forming and left the women feeling part of something very important. At the same time, however, it removed one of the formal vehicles that we had for getting together. In an almost spontaneous way, a smaller group of the women began meeting weekly for lunch.

"We got together and simply began to share the information that we had. For instance, a woman working in one of the business offices would share information that she had about budget cuts that were coming or new organizations that were being formed. If one woman was having a problem, the others would share from their own experiences about what to do or who to see. Some of the conversation was just rowdy and raucous. The group decided to call itself SLUG. The *S* was never defined, but the LUG was Ladies Underground. We'd use this name to send out information to each other. The men in the organization were incredibly curious and anxious, and sometimes terrified, especially those higher up in the organization, or in personnel or human relations. There was virtually no part of the company that we didn't have covered. And we were perceived as this radical group who had pissed off top management. It was great fun. We loved it. Over time our group became very close and developed into a social group as well. It was a powerful support group, because we all knew and understood the work environment we were in and had also known each other long enough to have a sense of one another's personal situations. There was simply unconditional support among us, even though we were all quite different. As a result of this support and SLUG, the careers of the women in this group thrived. It was incredible."

There are women in our lives who are like Jo in *Little Women*. Sometimes she is one woman alone, sometimes a group. Jo was good hearted, but not afraid to step in a little mud. And that is what we learn to respect in our girlfriends. They are strong when things are really messy, when we are snarling, raging, or mourning, when we are finding new courage in ourselves. They stride right into the muck and take the situation in hand. Sometimes it is the intensity of the muck which really establishes the friendship. All we may need is one friend to share her strength, and we can become clear-headed and courageous again.

Surviving Betrayal

Forgiveness is the act of admitting we are like other people.

—CHRISTINA BALDWIN

Being lied to or betrayed by a friend can be bewildering and cut you adrift from your usual moorings. Our friends are so important to us that when one of them deserts us, we miss her terribly. Not only does the betrayal hurt, but we have lost the person to whom we would normally have gone for comfort.

Emily, in her midthirties, still feels badly that she didn't tell her high school friend that their other friends were talking about her. "My friend was in the Junior Miss pageant, and our other friends got jealous of her and started saying she was really stuck up and she thought she was going to win. I didn't say anything against her, but I didn't stand up for her either. I didn't tell her that they were saying that about her, and she found out and got upset. She really hated me. I would have, too, since we were best friends. I really felt terrible about it. In fact, I still do, even though she got over it eventually."

With this kind of betrayal, we can usually fight, apologize, and with the passage of time, get over it. The kind of betrayal where someone just removes herself from the friendship seems impossible to fix; both parties have to want it.

Part of being a good friend and having good friends is being willing to stay in there and fight. But sometimes we discover that a friend would rather leave us than fight with us. Wendy, a professor, described her hurt and disappointment when her friend Donna pulled out of her life without explanation. She said, "I was very close to Donna and I still feel very fond of her, but I consider what happened with her a kind of betrayal. Evidently, she became very angry first with my husband and then with me. Instead of telling us what angered her and giving us a chance to resolve it, she simply disappeared. At the time, she and her husband were people that we saw regularly—once or twice a month for dinner or a movie, even going away for the weekend together. I guess she was expecting that my husband and I would respond by calling her and saying, 'What's wrong, what's wrong?' I think that people who handle their anger like that are just fundamentally untrustworthy. I won't tolerate it, and I experience it as a betrayal of the connection. You have to have enough respect for maintaining this connection to at least call and say, 'I'm really angry at you, I'm so angry at you that I don't even want to talk to you.' If someone doesn't have at least that much respect, then I can't take the risk to be connected."

Many of the stories we heard about girlfriends betraying one another included a man. Few betrayals hurt as much as finding out your close girlfriend has been involved with your boyfriend. Dana talked about when her best friend violated her trust: "I was just out of high school and in love with Brad, a guy I'd been seeing for about six months. I was very excited because this was a new kind of relationship for me; he was a lover.

"Brad, my best friend, and I were hanging out one time. He reached over and moved a hair from her face and, pow! I just knew that they were lovers! I hadn't suspected a thing, but that movement and the way he did it convinced me. When Brad and I went home, I confronted him and he denied it for about an hour. Then he copped to it.

"I didn't know how to handle it. Eventually I went over to my friend's house with a twelve-pack of beer. When she opened the door, I said, 'You know, we really need to talk.' She immediately broke down. We talked about it, and it felt so good to have it right out there. A year and a half later I was maid of honor at her wedding. We're still close."

Betrayal not only is painful to the woman betrayed, it is also difficult for the woman who has been the betrayer. Cathy described to us what it felt like to betray her friend. She confessed, "When Melissa and I were college roommates, she was dating a guy she adored. I don't know why I did it—I guess because I was young and full of myself—but I started seeing him on the side and pretending I wasn't. Of course, eventually she found out and was crushed by it.

"We talked about it, and it hurt to know I'd hurt her. In fact, to this day I suspect I feel worse about it than she does. We survived that, because she forgave me and we're still close friends. She lives in Chicago and I in California, but I still consider her one of my closest friends."

Most women who discussed betrayal said also that forgiveness could be had. Many women found that they could forgive their friends easier than their lovers. Elise, sales director for a distributor, commented, "People aren't so hard on their friends. If they were as easy on their mates as they were on their friends, their love relationships would go much better! I even got angry and called my friend Leslie a liar once, and we laugh at that now. I think it's because we have so many good memories together."

Friends can betray one another through actions and words that hurt the other's feelings, but friends must be careful to not go *looking* for betrayal. A friend is not looking for your faults and does not set up situations where you can disappoint her. As Holly, in her late thirties, wrote, "I value that we take care of our friendships. I make sure that I am understood and that I understand. I'm not hurtful, and I don't look for ways to feel hurt."

In a situation of betrayal, we recommend the "most generous" test. Try to apply either the standard of forgiveness you would apply to your friend or the standard of forgiveness you would apply to yourself, whichever is the most generous. When betrayal does occur, forgiveness is the only path back to friendship.

Being Heard

If you want to be listened to, you should put in time listening.

—MARGE PIERCY

There was no way for me to understand it at the time, but the talk that filled the kitchen those afternoons was highly functional. It served as therapy, the cheapest kind available to my mother and her friends. . . . But more than therapy, that freewheeling, wide-ranging, exuberant talk functioned as an outlet for the tremendous creative energy they possessed.

—PAULE MARSHALL

Miraculously, our most serious situations seem to lighten when we tell them to a friend and feel that she has heard us. The magic happens when a friend is able to put herself in our place and, knowing us as she does, to help us come to a decision without necessarily solving the problem for us. Being heard is a clarifying potion—not made by any cosmetics company—that helps us to see things clearly. Cheryl, a teacher and mother of two, commented, "Until you've actually bounced an idea off another friend, you can't clarify it in your mind."

Tamara, one of the authors, described it this way: "I tend to see problems as two dimensional—huge, flat moviescreen images coming at me. I think I see a problem and then I feel that the problem must be my fault somehow, so there is this added sense of shame or guilt around the situation. It is overwhelming. I can escape from this downward spiral in an emotional emergency by calling all of my friends and talking over the problem with each of them. Just the fact that I am saying it out loud to each of them helps me to view the situation more realistically. And their responses each add a level of perspective and wisdom that allows me to see a different view of the problem. The problem, whatever it is, becomes life-size instead of larger than life, and I start seeing it in perspective. It makes the problem three dimensional, if you will, and therefore deflatable."

Suzy, a poet now living in suburban Connecticut, underscores the importance of having a good friend listen to us with this story: "At one point in my life, I married a former boyfriend who lived on the West Coast. I left New York and a middle-class life to become a hippie, living with Jon on a commune in the remote woods of northern California with no phone and no electricity. Karen and I started corresponding. Those letters, the slower process of reflection and writing, created another level of intimacy between us. I would write to her during those 2 A.M. hours of insomnia when marital or work anxiety beset me. Sometimes I wouldn't mail them, although I started each letter 'Dear Karen' with her eyes and ears as the intended audience. Somehow, just thinking she might read what I was writing calmed me. After I'd poured out my feelings on paper, I'd feel able to return to bed."

The necessity of having a listening friend is illustrated by Anne Frank's story. Anne, locked in her hideaway, did not have a girlfriend, so she made one up, her diary. As Patricia Hampl wrote about the new definitive edition of the diary released in spring of 1995, "From the first, she addressed the notebook as a trusted girlfriend: 'I'll begin from the moment I got you, the moment I saw you lying on the table among my other birthday presents.' A few days later this anonymous 'you' becomes the imaginary 'Kitty,' and the entries turn into letters, giving the diary the intimacy and vivacity of a developing friendship."[13]

Clarity and perspective are what we gain from our friends who hear us, *really* hear us, who take the time to stop other tasks and focus on what we are saying. How powerful that act is, and how powerfully even imagining a friend listening, as Anne Frank and Suzy did, can affect us. High quality listening, even more so than high quality advice, can keep us grounded and help us listen to our own hearts, finding our answers within ourselves.

Acceptance

*Oh, the comfort, the inexpressible comfort of feeling safe with a
person, having neither to weigh thoughts nor measure words,
but pouring them all right out, just as they are, chaff and
grain together; certain that a faithful hand will take and
sift them, keep what is worth keeping, and then with the
breath of kindness blow the rest away.*

—DINAH MARIA MULOCK CRAIK

The best thing about girlfriends is that we can be whoever
we are with them, and they will accept us anyway. No per-
sona required, we can be cranky or perky—and both may
be annoying—with greasy hair and a sweater two sizes too
small that's covered with ugly little balls. It really does not
matter to our close friends what we look like or what mood
we're in. As Alice describes being with her friends, there
are "no holds barred, no image making or trying to live up
to an ideal." Cheryl observes, "When you're with your
really good friends you don't care what you look like. Each
year my friends and I take a trip away from our families. In
the mornings, everyone just walks around looking as
though they are eighty years old. No one is trying to
impress anyone else. Competition is not a part of our
friendship."

Judy Hart, the author of *Love, Judy: Letters of Hope and
Healing for Women With Breast Cancer,* most appreciates those
friends who are not afraid of her sickness and her feelings

around it. Having friends accept her in whatever mental and physical state she happens to be in is very important. "The most crucial form of friendship for me has been what I call my psyche friends. Obviously there are people who will do an errand for you or take you to an appointment, leave something on the doorstep, send something in the mail, telephone. But the women who have really made the difference for me are the ones I can talk to absolutely from where I am and who are not going to be shocked or tell me to feel better or give me advice. I'm most touched by those who have been courageous enough to share what my illness means to them.

"I guess opening up the passages is a lot of what I'm doing with the cancer, because I know it is a threatening subject, and I was brought up in a time, a place, a family where you're not supposed to talk about unpleasant things unless you can be upbeat. The image that I grew up with is people talking about somebody who lost her husband saying, 'Oh, she's just wonderful. She gets her hair done, she gets a nice suit of clothes, she takes a cruise to Europe, and she plays bridge with the girls.' What they really mean is that she's not making anyone uncomfortable that she's going through anything different or unusual or difficult. I'd rather be real, and a part of me inside says, 'Oh, you're breaking all the rules,' and then I watch how it does open up the passages. But I think this is what friendships and human relationships are all about — daring to keep open the passages."

By accepting characteristics of friends, we may find that we are achieving a balance in our own lives. Sue Thoele and Bonnie Hampton each feel that the other has brought some balance to her development. Bonnie noted, "I spent the formative years of my life, 1960 to 1981, in Berkeley, living an avant garde, California lifestyle. There was a kind of independence and toughness about me that Sue didn't have. There was an intuitive womanliness about her that I didn't have. We were able to tug each other into a balanced place around that. When we get out of balance we can reach out, and the other person helps balance that out. It's just completeness."

Sue continues, "What keeps coming up in my mind, because I am really visual, is the yin-yang symbol. When we met, I had an incredible amount of yin energy, and Bonnie had such an incredible amount of yang energy. We were imbalanced. Our relationship helped us stabilize and balance and harmonize those energies in ourselves."

By feeling accepted, we learn to like ourselves more. When we like ourselves more, we can accept others and be more patient of what we think of as their foibles. By being more accepting of our friends, we may bring some balance into our own lives. The cycle that friendship provides is a worthwhile one to begin.

She's Like Family

God gave us our relatives;
thank God we can choose our friends.

—ETHEL WATTS MUMFORD

An interesting paradox arises when we describe our friends. Often wishing to illustrate the seriousness of the friendship or the closeness we feel toward a friend, we use the phrase "she's like my sister" or "my friends are my family." Yet many of us would not share the details of our inner lives and outer occupations with our families the way we do with our best girlfriends. One woman described her relationship with her friends as a "feeling of going home that I don't have with my own parents, so I think I value that much more having a 'home' with certain friends."

Perhaps, as we get older and do not want to pass our worries on to our aging parents, we tend to share our burdens with friends. Social psychologist Lillian Rubin, in her book, *Just Friends,* adds another dimension to the contrast of family and friends by observing that in the family our earlier needs to be loved and accepted mesh with the family's earlier expectations of our younger selves. Roles that we played in our families can reemerge with family members, resisting all efforts to change them. With friends however, we can be seen as evolving, changing adults. "There's little doubt that, if a friendship is to survive and grow, it will usually serve us better in keeping us in touch with our adult self than do our relations in the family."[14] Having a sisterhood of friends can be especially poignant for women who have come from alcoholic or abusive families. One woman told us, "I have two younger sisters. I can be more honest with my friends. My sisters and I share a painful childhood that has brought us close, but there is too much history to really feel like successful adults together. My friends mirror my growth."

Nevertheless, there is a still a sacredness about family relationships. Rubin summarizes, "For most of us, kinship falls into the realm of the sacred, friendship into the arena of the secular. There's a mystique about kin relations, a sense of awe about them, a belief that these relationships, although not necessarily the people themselves, transcend ordinary considerations and everyday feelings."[15] Some women resolve this seeming contradiction by making their friends their family. "Family" seems to connote a higher level of commitment and an ability to give much as well as expect much.

The poet Maya Angelou signifies this level of commitment by "making sisters" with her closest friends. In an interview with the authors of *The Feminine Face of God*, Angelou explains:

A sister is no plaything. . . . You have to consider. You have to talk about it. After you're friends and you see that you have so much in common and you love each other, you ask, "Could we be sisters?" If the person says yes, you repeat together, "You really are my sister." And then you go about informing both of your families. . . . Now her brothers are my brothers, and our two families are joined. And I have other sisters as well. . . . In times of trouble, there are about seven women in the United States I can call at any hour and say "Now. Now. I need you now." And they will come. No questions. No objections. . . . Nothing, nothing would keep them from me and me from them.[16]

Some women have combined friendships with family ties by encouraging a girlfriend to marry into the family. Catherine, from North Carolina, writes, "Nancy and I met in New York in 1948 when we both attended college. We had rooms near each other in the hotel where the students lived and were also in the same class in school. Something clicked between us almost immediately. Even though she was from North Carolina and I was from New Jersey, we found that we had many things in common.

"As I didn't live very far from New York, I was able to go home on weekends, and frequently Nancy came with me. She soon became part of my family and the sister that I never had. My brother was engaged when I met Nancy, and after my father got to know her he often said he wished he had another son to marry Nancy! When I visited her family, I found that I, too, fit right in.

"I married soon after graduating and moved to Pennsylvania, while Nancy stayed in New York. However, we kept in touch, and when I moved to Long Island several years later, we were able to get together fairly often. During the year we lived on Long Island, I introduced her to my cousin, and within a year they were married, so we really did become family. Of course this was the next best thing to my father's wish that she marry a son of his!"

With families we expect unconditional acceptance. However, many of the women we interviewed did not feel their families accept them as they are. Many have found that needed level of acceptance with their friends. If we say our friends are like our families, we mean we share the highest level of commitment to and acceptance of each other, even if our families do not, in reality, meet our needs or our expectations.

Our Mothers and Friendship

My mother is a poem I'll never be able to write
Though everything I write is a poem to my mother.

—TILLIE OLSEN

Many of our girlfriends provide some link to that other important woman in our lives, our mother. Some friends we interviewed met because their mothers were friends, some bonded because they had similar problems with their mothers, and some women have first experienced, then learned, the art of friendship from their mothers.

Seventy-three-year-old Rachel Anne talked about how the friendship between her mother and her friend Joyce's mother adds another dimension to their own friendship.

"My longest-term girlfriend is somebody that I knew from the time we were preschoolers and our mothers belonged to the same club. She still lives in the same house that she lived in when she and I were children, whereas I have moved all over and I see her seldom. Thinking and talking about friendships prompted me to call her, and we started the conversation just as if we'd seen each other the day before yesterday. Our friendship is different now than it was ever before, however, because we talked about our mothers' friendship with one another.

"Joyce said of her mother, 'My mother had a heart as big as a washtub,' and I said of my mother, 'My mother was a very simple, plain person, with a heart of gold.' It was her mother that arranged that Joyce take me from the school bus into the kindergarten room on the first day of school. Interestingly, Joyce became a kindergarten teacher, and I became an early childhood educator and a teacher of teachers. I don't think we had ever hit upon the importance of our mothers' friendship, but in that conversation, we remembered and celebrated that lifelong friendship. It was a whole other dimension that I hadn't thought about."

Jeannie and Isobel grew up in the Midwest and have been friends for over thirty years. "Whenever we talk about our friendship, we find ourselves talking about each other's mother, because when we were little kids we were always around and affected not only by our own mother, but also by the other's mother. When the two of us get together now, it's almost like there are four of us. Dorothy and Betty are there. I see their faces all the time when we are together. I see the little things they kept around the house, like the amber-colored ashtray set on the coffee table and the serving plate with raised white dots on it."

Perhaps one reason women need women friends so desperately is that only another woman can understand from the inside the relationship that a daughter and mother have and the power of that relationship to mold, comfort, irritate, support, or devastate one. Angela, a graphic designer, gave this example: "I really believe that the reason my girlfriends, particularly Kim, have been so important to me is because they are the only people who can really understand the relationship between my mother and me. My mother calls me every day, which I was afraid to admit to anyone. So when Kim and I discussed being roommates, I was too embarrassed to tell her about my mother's calls. Consequently, I lived by myself for many years.

"Years later I found out that Kim's mother calls her every day, so I didn't have to be embarrassed after all. My girlfriends are really the only people that can understand that relationship. Since the relationship with your mother is so key to who you are, and it changes so much throughout your life, having a girlfriend is essential survival equipment."

Helen, an author, found that she needed her lifelong friend as a witness to Helen's relationship with her mother: "Mary and I have been friends since we were in fifth grade. We know each other's mothers very well. For almost all of my life, I lived in this cloud of denial about my family. Mary was able to tell me, I guess about eight years ago, that it was hard for her to watch the mothering that went on in my family. She didn't say anything until I had gotten into therapy and had worked out some things about my family, and it was very shocking to hear this from a witness. However, it was also very wonderful to hear it from a witness, because it validated some of the feelings that I had been having about what had gone on in my family. It helped me to see those relationships more clearly. I really appreciate her honesty."

On the other end of the spectrum, our mothers can teach us how to be caring and supportive friends by their own examples, and they can provide us with our first and foremost friendship. Thirteen-year-old Tara, when talking about her lifelong friends, listed several and then concluded, "I did forget one lifelong girlfriend; she is my very, very best friend. We have been friends so long that she was at my birth. Actually, she performed my birth! That's right, it's good old Mom. I know I can tell her anything and she won't tell anyone. She is always there to lend a hand to get up with or a shoulder to cry on. I just don't know what I'd do without her, my very best, very special friend."

Betsy, a mother of four living in St. Louis, finds that her relationship with her mother has been her most enduring and gratifying friendship. "Of all the friendships with women that I have, the one that I most cherish, that is most regular, most sustaining, and most satisfying is the friendship with my mother. I can't articulate all the facets of our friendship, but they are deep, abiding, spiritual, intellectual, and long-standing. My mother is one of nine children, eight of whom were girls. She lived most of her youth surrounded by women, both in all-girls' boarding and day schools and with her many sisters. She grew up in a time when children were to be seen and not heard, which pushed her and her sisters into a secret society of sorts. To this day she and her sisters talk and correspond what I think is an amazing amount considering they range in age from sixty-five to eighty.

"She has always cared deeply about social issues, about the intellectual life, about culture. That's probably the single biggest reason we are so close; we have things and ideas that have carried us through our various stages in life.

"During motherhood, her friendship and support have sustained me like no other female relationship. There's never been a day when I couldn't call her and say, 'The kids are driving me nuts!' to which she always responds, 'Throw 'em in the car and c'mon over.' At those moments when my emotional well has all but dried up, there she is, feeding them ginger ale mixed with cranberry juice—with straws, of course, in soda shop Coca-Cola glasses—and her own private mix of goldfish crackers, wheat thins and peanuts. They are refreshed; I glut on the *New York Times* and all kinds of reading matter that overflows the coffee table. At other times, it's dress-up with real lipstick, real rouge, the works.

"At her most generous moments, she will look at me holding one of my children and say, 'I didn't hold my babies enough.' Or, 'If I had to do it again, I'd have nursed all my children.' All children know the healing effects of such an admission, unsolicited, from parent to child. And really, from friend to friend."

No relationship affects us more than our relationship with our mother. If that relationship has been painful, it may be several decades before a daughter can trust other women or appreciate women friends. Certainly good women friends will be required to heal that pain. If that primary relationship with mother is positive, however, we learn how to be good women and good friends at the same time. Or are these the same thing?

Sisters

Both within the family and without, our sisters hold up our mirrors, our images of who we are and of who we can dare to become.

—ELIZABETH FISHEL

The subject of sisters seems so complicated that we hesitated to delve into it at all. But we wanted to hear how sister relationships differ, if at all, from relationships with girlfriends. We found when we asked women who have sisters to compare their relationships with their friends to their relationships with their sisters, we received a whole range of responses, from genuine enthusiasm to severe sadness and disappointment. On the one hand, women recognized the ability of sisters to know them like no one else can. As Margie says of her sister Ruth, "When she's telling me the truth I feel like she really knows what she's talking about because she knows everything about me from the very beginning." On the other hand, women expressed ambivalence when speaking about their sisters. Ruth summed it up best when she spoke about Margie: "I feel in some ways like Margie is my best friend and in some ways not. I have a lot of women friends whom I value very much and am very close to, but still, I don't have to stay if a relationship is not working. I can leave it behind if necessary. But Margie and I are different because we're sisters, we're always going to be sisters, we're always going to have that connection.

"We've always been together, and she's been an enormous factor in my life because of everything that happened in our family. I've gone through years of therapy and twelve-step programs to try and heal from things that happened in the family. One of the things that really kept me going was knowing that Margie valued me."

Some women we interviewed were estranged from their sisters. Judy told us, "My family never talked about anything, so it's hard for me to talk about things." She began crying. "I can't talk to my sister, because she's closed, too. It's so hard for us to express anything. But I find I can talk with my friends and tell them things that are going on about me. But not my sister. It's really sad."

Hanna, forty-six, was able to establish a good relationship with her sisters, although it took a great deal of effort. She said, "I have two sisters, both younger. We didn't become friends until years after we moved from our parents' home. In our family, the focus was on my father and his illness or his insanity, depending on what day it was. We didn't relate to each other much, and it's taken years for us to see each other as individuals in our own lives. It took a lot of conversation, a lot of letters, because it meant something to us to keep an adult friendship and not have it fall apart as my parents died and became infirm."

Similarly, Jennifer, now in her early twenties, didn't develop a friendship with her sister until they were adults. She told us, "I'm very, very close to my sister now, but I think that we only started becoming friends after we both moved out of our house, so then being friends became a choice. When we were at home we fought all the time and we were very competitive. But once we started forming our own identities away from the family we chose to be friends. Now we get along really well, and I consider her a good friend. I really don't see that much difference between my friendship with her and my friendship with my other friends. I'm just as open with her as with my friends, if not more so."

Sister seems to imply so much—on the one hand, a potentially devastating, sad relationship of discord and regret, and on the other, a closeness that no other relationship can offer. When we discussed the topic of girlfriends with writer Sue Monk Kidd, she theorized, "The most profound female friendships often emerge out of women who were unsistered. I think the need for sisters is innate. Out of that need, we spend our lives looking for a sister surrogate." Whether we have sisters or not, we look for the archetype of the sister, the woman who knows us better than anyone, who shares everything with us, who loves us as a blood relation. These are our girlfriends.

Saving Our Lives

Does that mean I never let her down? Does that mean the rhythm is always in step? It means that in spite of, or including these issues, I absolutely can count on her. And what is so valuable is that I don't believe that is open to question.

—CATHERINE SMITH, PH.D.

We have heard many stories about girlfriends saving each other's lives, most often figuratively and sometimes literally. Anne, a childhood educator now retired, tells this story about how a friend helped her in her career: "I was studying at the University of Iowa and was finishing up my master's thesis. I was getting ready to move to the East Coast, and although I had finished my course work and written the thesis, I was running out of time before I moved, and the thesis needed to be typed. I knew I would not finish it once I was out of the school environment, because I just knew I would become distracted. I don't ever remember asking her for help, but my friend Carolyn showed up— she was an excellent typist—and typed my thesis. If she hadn't typed it, I would not have finished my master's degree. That act of friendship has made a big difference in my life, as the master's degree opened doors that would not have opened without it."

Elizabeth, thirty-five, told us another story where she received the help she needed without having to ask. "Kim called one morning a few years ago just to check in on things. When one of my children answered and said, 'Mommy's sick,' Kim immediately got in her car, drove over, and picked up and kept my three small children for the day. I was too sick even to argue, and she knew it."

Roberta, a secretary in her thirties, tells this story: "When I attempted suicide and came out of it, the first person I saw was Colleen crying. I asked her why she was crying, and she replied something like, 'Because you're here in the hospital.' I don't recall anyone else being there; I'm sure they were around, but not when I became conscious. Colleen is really great, very strong and supportive, discreet and very diplomatic, and for her to cry really means she cared a lot whether I lived. She is not very emotionally forthright—I don't think she ever cried in front of me when her grandmother or father died—so her emotion meant a lot to me. Suddenly I understood that what I did had had an effect on her. Up until then I was just thinking how I would like to leave the planet, not really thinking of the consequences for family and friends around me."

Asked how she thought Colleen's presence helped her get through that difficult time in her life, Roberta replied, "Colleen was a really good friend to me. It was hard for me to explain why I was so depressed, but she would never push for answers, explanations. She just helped me by listening, always without judgment and criticism. And she would always be there to take me to the doctor, to listen for hours on the phone, and so forth. I must have been a pain in the neck."

Sometimes we are rescued by our friends just staying with us, as we swirl around in a crisis or tiptoe over a slick, glassy place in our lives. The following story, which Sue told, provides the perfect metaphor for so many of the situations in which our friends save our lives. Sue, an author, began, "Betty and I were having a picnic by a river, and I had this bright idea that we should walk across the river to the other side. So we took our shoes off and tied them together, threw them over our shoulders, rolled up our pants, and started across. I went first and got about halfway when I realized the currents were stronger than they looked. I lost my balance somewhat and my shoes fell off my shoulders. I thought, 'I'm going to get those shoes, they cost eighty dollars.'

"So I went after the shoes, and Betty was still on the bank. I was taken by the current and getting in over my head fast—literally. I realized about forty yards downriver that I may not get those shoes. In fact, perhaps I wouldn't get out myself! Betty was running as fast as she could along the riverbank with me, somehow managing to keep up. She stayed with me every bit of the way saying, 'I'm with you, I'm with you. Hang in there, I'll get you!'

"She found a long branch, which I finally grabbed and got out. But I'll always remember her running along, saying, 'I'm with you.' That captures something about unconditional love between women. It's an enduring tie we know we have."

Outlasting Transition

*It has begun to occur to me that life is a stage
I'm going through.*

—ELLEN GOODMAN

Life's one invariable is that everything changes. We change
as people, we gain and lose jobs, husbands, lovers, children. New faces and personalities drift into and sometimes
out of our lives. Friendships can take a beating in these
times of transition. However, any friendship that survives
will be all the stronger and even more precious.

Weddings and All That Goes with Them

A wedding invitation is beautiful and formal notification of the desire to share a solemn and joyous occasion, sent by people who have been saying "Do we have to ask them?" to people whose first response is "How much do you think we have to spend on them?"

—MISS MANNERS

Weddings mark a major transition in a woman's life, regardless of the age of the bride. The decision to marry and the portent of the corresponding responsibilities are very serious matters that, at the very least, can make you a bit nervous and, at the most, make you wish to be abducted by aliens to live on the mother ship for the rest of your natural days. Have we mentioned the expectations of parents (both bride's and groom's) and their respective friends, the logistics of getting two hundred people to your hometown (or just from the church to the reception), and the free and certainly unsolicited advice that everyone feels obligated to share with a woman about to be married? Add to that the centuries of tradition and assumptions wrapped around the act of marriage (women as property, only virgins are acceptable, a woman's greatest achievement is to land a man), assumptions that keep showing up in the rituals (another man "giving you away," the white dress, the throwing of the bouquet to the "eager" bridesmaids), and a woman is in for what used to be called a nervous break-down. Even those valiant women of any age who are deter-mined to keep their wedding just the way they want it, without including guests, rituals, or traditions that they don't like, spend enormous amounts of time and emotional effort defending their wishes. If you haven't gone through this yourself, we recommend watching the Australian film *Muriel's Wedding* to get an idea of what expectations and stakes are involved in a wedding.

If you never needed your girlfriends before, you need them *now*, if for no other reason than to keep you sane and perhaps even laughing. On the day of Isabella's wedding, which was to take place in her family home, she was suffer-ing from "the jitters." As she watched the guests arrive, her anxiety increased exponentially, and she describes herself as feeling like "a total basket case." Before the ceremony, she was pacing around in her bridal gown, wringing her hands and chattering nervously. Compounding her ner-vous state was her grief that her father, who had died a few years before, was going to miss this day. She felt his absence intensely at this important event in her life.

Isabella's friend, who had just flown in for the wedding, watched as Isabella stalked around the room and made wild statements that made no sense. Then, as Isabella recalls, "She commanded me to sit down and start making a bouquet out of the various bows and ribbons which were thrown around the room from presents people had brought me. Making a bouquet from the ribbons sounded like a strange idea, but in my state of panic, I did it anyway. Because she knew me so well, she knew exactly what I needed at that moment and because I trusted her I did it — even though it was really silly. But it seemed to work. As I sat there with my friend and made that bouquet, I felt calmer. And as I began noticing what I was doing, I realized how ridiculous the whole scene was. I looked at my friend and we both started laughing uproariously, allowing me then to talk about my sadness over my father's absence. All the pain and panic were released so I could walk down the aisle in peace."

Girlfriends are often asked to carry out tasks at the wedding other than calming the bride. Usually they do these tasks eagerly. There is something especially sweet about friends helping with all the details. But sometimes even the best of intentions backfire. One woman, normally a competent attorney, related everyone's worst nightmare: "I was supposed to pack the bride's overnight bag, but I had too much champagne at the reception and forgot to pack her birth control pills. The horrible thing was that they were traveling to some obscure place for their honeymoon, and she sent me a telegram saying, 'Gee, thanks for forgetting the birth control pills. We'll name the baby after you.' Somehow she did not get pregnant. I was so relieved."

Another woman assigned her girlfriends the task of gathering wildflowers for all the banquet tables. It's a lovely image, isn't it — this woman's closest friends out in the fields of Maine, gathering real wildflowers for the tables? Unfortunately, one detail was forgotten. Emily relates the story: "We forgot to spray the flowers for bugs, so all the banquet tables had bugs crawling all over them!"

And some of the assigned tasks we can ask only our dearest and most committed of friends to endure on our special day. For example, one woman spent protracted lengths of time in the hotel deep freeze searching for the bride's flowers, which had been misplaced. Another was dispatched to beg the aunt-in-law-from-hell to come out of her hotel room to the wedding.

Carmen, one of the authors, tells her most memorable wedding story: "I was the maid of honor, and we were all up there watching the bride and groom do the candle-lighting ritual—you know, where they each take a lighted candle and light a third one together. The candles had metal covers over them to keep them from dripping, and Carolyn, the bride, had trouble getting her candle out of the holder. She struggled and struggled, and, as people started to giggle, she braced her feet wide apart and ripped that candle out of the holder. She then regrouped and very daintily lit the center candle with the groom.

"I felt a tap on my shoulder, and I looked back to see the bridesmaid behind me pointing to the floor. To my horror, I saw that her train was smoldering into flames. Apparently when the bride had flung the candle out of the holder, the candle itself had flown out of the metal sheath. Here was the burning candle, on the bride's train, about to set my dear friend on fire!

"I threw my bouquet to the floor, got down on my hands and knees, and frantically pounded out the fire. Then I picked up my bouquet and acted like nothing had happened. After the ceremony we explained the burn hole in her dress and Carolyn said, 'I wondered what the snickering was about! Thanks for saving my life!' I think that lifesaving goes well beyond the call of duty in being a bridesmaid."

Speaking of bridesmaids, there seems to be one phenomenon that we have all experienced with our girlfriends that no one has explained to our satisfaction: bridesmaid dresses. We all know what we are talking about here. What is it that possesses intelligent women of normally good taste when it comes to this matter? Has anyone not been horrified when shown the chosen pattern? Ask any woman about weddings in which she has attended the bride, and her eyes will roll up in her head, she will shudder, and her next words will be, "You would not believe this dress. . . ."

Here are some of our favorite designs that women described to us: a purple, sparkly, one-shouldered number with a big flower at the hip (perfect for every figure); red velvet with white fur trim and muff (for that holiday wedding); green quiana (the fabric with no weave) with matching hat; pink, taffeta Laura Ashley-style with a big bow on the butt (for the inner child); burgundy velvet with a capelet (that's a little cape, so you can look like one of the March sisters), and, last but not least, a Little Bo Peep dress with a parasol (you can use it again when you are gathering sheep). We are sure every woman has her own horror story.

One woman tells this tale: "My friend Laura asked her girlfriends to sew their own bridesmaids' dresses and then picked out this hideous pattern—one I am convinced was designed to make her look like a million bucks. There were pleats down the front, and each person's pleats, depending on the seamstress, was a huge zigzag, and when she saw us she exclaimed, 'Can't you sew straight? You're going to ruin my wedding!' She made us carry our flowers at the chest level to cover up the lines."

We heard of another bridesmaid (this may be a myth) who found her dress so hideous that she refused to wear it to the reception. She drove straight from the church to the dumpster in the church parking lot to rip the dress off and throw it away.

We have a theory based on a comment that one woman made about her plans for her own wedding. With a strange gleam in her eye, she smiled and said, "If I ever get married, my plan is to make my bridesmaids wear the last five dresses that I have had to wear to my friends' weddings." Perhaps there is some continuing, unconscious cycle of revenge that is happening here. Every woman has had to humiliate herself before large groups of people to satisfy their girlfriends' desires. Usually this is done with only a minimal amount of muttering and grumbling—especially when buying yet another pair of satin shoes to dye turquoise. Yet when we get married—aaaahhhh, revenge!

Children and Changes

Nothing is more dependable than a child's digestive juices.

—RENEE HAWKLEY

Becoming a mother is certainly a major challenge for most women. We need other women to instruct us, support us, and invent ways to survive the many joyous and frightening aspects of parenting. Cheryl, a homemaker and middle school teacher, talked to us about her group of girlfriends: "The fascinating thing is that we have gone through life's stages together. First we all were young, had young husbands and partied a lot. Then we had babies. The kids became teenagers and we all moaned about that. Now we are facing empty nests and dealing with college expenses.

"The best thing is that just when you think your child is warped or something's going wrong or that you're a lousy parent, you talk about it in the group and somebody else laughs and says, 'Oh, I went through that,' or, 'My child went through that.' It affirms the fact that parenthood is a roller-coaster ride. Everybody experiences both the good and the bad moments. It helps to know that we all face high and low points and that not one of us had a perfect child."

Similarly, the experience of bringing up children together and watching each other's children develop and affect each other intertwines women's hearts and memories even more. Anne, in her early seventies, talks about a friend, Gretchen: "Some of my closest friends at this point in my life are people who have seen our children grow up and I've seen their children grow up. One particular friend and I traveled together in recent years, whereas for many years we were just so involved with children — she had five and I had six — that we very seldom saw each other. However, we kept in touch and knew what each other's children were doing across the country.

"There's something very wonderful, at this point in my life, about Gretchen being able to say, 'Remember that time when the girls were two, three, and five and I took care of them while you planned the house?' We remember the long-term experience. I remember one of our girls admired one of her boys when we both lived in the South and he refused to sing 'Dixie' in class. This was in a county neighboring a county that had closed all its schools to avoid desegregation. As the years have gone by, it's really precious to us that our children had some very deep, meaningful experiences together."

When mothers are friends, they can share childcare, taking pride in each other's children and providing each other a needed respite. As Susan said about her friend Jeanette and herself, "I think we both feel that we are kind of surrogate mothers to each other's kids. I feel very comfortable having my kids in her care. I always feel comfortable that whatever decision she makes to discipline them is the same decision that I would make myself. I think she feels that way about me as well." This shared parenting bolsters the fabric of their friendship even more.

Girlfriends also provide the valuable service of being able to hear your complaints about your children without misunderstanding. Bonnie described how her friendship with Sue has been essential in the rearing of her own children. "I've always felt that I could say anything to Sue about my children, and she would always understand that it never diminished how much I loved them and adored them. We don't have to backtrack and add 'And you know how much I really love this child.' The given in any conversation is that the other one is holding that love for the child. While I struggled with something, Sue could remember for me how much I adored that child. Similarly, I could remind Sue that her child was perfect in a certain way while she was struggling with an imperfection. There's no betrayal of the child in the discussion with each other, because the other mother, the one who's capable of being the good-enough mother in the moment, is there holding the good-enough part of the child."

While shared motherhood can strengthen some relationships, other friendships can become strained if one woman in the dyad is childless. Stella, a travel agent, recalled when Traci had her first child, her whole perspective changed. "We used to talk about current events, travel together, and share career goals. Suddenly she could talk for hours, it seemed, about diapers and breast feeding and stuff completely foreign to me. I didn't feel like I fit in any more."

When we talked with Traci, she expressed disappointment in the distance that developed between herself and

Stella after her first child was born. Traci told us, "I tried to stay connected and share what I was experiencing. But the more I shared, the more distant she became. I guess we couldn't make the transition."

Faith, the mother of twins, and her friend, Tina, who has no children, told us quite a different story. Faith said, "Tina was a major support throughout my pregnancy and understood I was going through a major change. Once my husband and I got the hang of our new schedule, Tina and I got together once a week just like before."

Tina affirmed, "I don't know if I'll ever have children of my own so it was a thrill to go through Faith's pregnancy with her. Everything fascinated me.

"I think Faith's husband helped us stay connected after the babies were born. He was very supportive of my coming over and watched the boys so Faith and I would have some time together. I am really glad to have all of them in my life."

Based on Faith and Tina's experience, friendship can survive children, even if one friend has none. It depends on whether both women are eager to stay connected, and stretch to meet the new circumstances. Having a spouse or partner to share the parenting duties helps as well.

Perhaps one of the most treasured aspects of motherhood is investing in the future through the lives of your children. As Gelsey Kirkland, a well-known American dancer, commented, "Fortunately for children, the uncertainties of the present always give way to the enchanted possibilities of the future."[17] Girlfriends who share in motherhood not only share today's struggles with one another, they also join in a most valuable contribution to the future.

Surviving Loss

*Oh Dear! how unfortunate I am not to have anyone
to weep with!*

—MADAME DE SÉVIGNÉ (c. 1670)

At moments of our deepest grief, women who have shared our experience can give us uniquely satisfying comfort. Lida, now in her sixties, told us about how her girlfriend, Dorothy, turned to Lida and her mother when Dorothy miscarried her first child. Lida said, "Dorothy was in her first trimester of pregnancy and had noticed some spotting one evening. Her husband was out of town, she lived out in the country, and she was scared. She instinctively turned to my mother, because Momma had had miscarriages and knew all the resulting emotions and fears Dorothy was experiencing. I had just had a baby, and Dorothy knew I would understand the love for an unborn baby. They talked, those two women I loved dearly, of the 'ifs, maybes, and whys,' then the 'hows and wherefores,' as Momma explained what was going to happen and I watched the clock. I cry to this day when I recall that night thirty-five years ago. We three women, two young, the other old, all trying to be adult in our understanding of life. She lost that baby. We all did. About a year later she had a daughter, and the wheel of love keeps turning."

When a crisis hits us, we are often knocked off balance and bruised by the fall. Having a girlfriend there to give us a private place to heal can make all the difference. As Marlene Dietrich said, "It is the friends you can call up at 4 A.M. that matter."[18] Priscilla, formerly a church administrator, remembers how, several years ago when she lost her job unexpectedly, she called her friend Elisabeth to tell her the news: "Elisabeth immediately said, 'Well, you know, Priscilla, if you want to live here with us, you can.' I packed up and went.

"When I got off the plane I was visibly depressed. In the car, Elisabeth said, 'Priscilla, this is not a time when you need to show up for anybody. So, when we get to the house, I'm going to show you where everything is, and if you choose to have your meals with us, fine. We eat at six. If you choose to remain in your room, that's fine. I'll bring a tray to you upstairs. Sleep whenever you want to sleep. If you want to spend the whole night writing, do that. If you want to go to church with us, that's fine. But if you're not speaking to God right now, that's fine, too. So far as money goes, it's not an issue. We've made our attic into your space, and you can stay for a year. Stay as long as you like.'

"I had this sense, in the car, that she didn't expect anything from me. 'We don't need to cheer you up or need you to get well or need to talk this through with you. Just be whatever you need to be.' What an incredibly loving gift."

Loving gifts from girlfriends are needed whenever we face a loss, most certainly when we lose someone we love through death. Patty, a mom herself, relates, "When I lost my mom unexpectedly after bypass surgery, I thought my world had come to an end. All of my good friends kept checking on me. They either called or stopped by with words of encouragement. This was very important to me and kept me going." Allison, a flower warehouse manager, has also turned to a friend in a difficult time: "The last three months have been difficult; I've been very depressed. My friend Shawn has always been there for me when I couldn't turn to anyone else, even my family!"

In times of loss, girlfriends can help us laugh in the midst of our sadness. Kathleen, a graphic designer in her early thirties, told us a story about how she and some other girl-friends helped a mutual friend face her first night alone without her husband. When a friend of Kathleen's sepa-rated from her husband and moved to a new place, "We had a whole gaggle of women over and had a slumber party. We bought and ate every food that you can imagine that is terrible for you — pop-tarts for breakfast, chocolate cookie dough by the spoonful. We watched *The Women* and just had a grand old time. There was camaraderie and laughter."

One of life's most moving experiences is having a friend entrust us with the pain they feel. In fact, if we were excluded from caring for our girlfriends in times of need, we'd feel left out or cheated somehow. Somehow the laws of gravity are suspended with sharing such a burden. The burden of loss that is shared is lightened by the sharing of it, yet the one who picks up part of the load is not burdened in the same measure. We feel honored to share the weight of a girlfriend's grief.

Picking Up Where We Left Off

Though our communication wanes at times of absence,
I'm aware of a strength that emanates in the background.

—CLAUDETTE RENNER

You know your friendship has withstood the test of time if you can pick up your conversation right where you left off, no matter how long it has been. As Elizabeth, a secretary, says of Jeanette, her friend of twenty-six years, "Despite moving all over the world, living in different countries, we can still stay up late at night discussing our lives, loves, and fears—pick up the conversation from where we left off!"

Laurie, a graduate student, says it doesn't matter how different are the paths that her close college friends have taken in their lives. "I feel like we've grown up together. Over the years, things have changed. We have taken different paths, some of which led to marriage and children or living in distant parts of the country. These changes have affected the quantity of time spent together, and whether time is spent in person or over the phone, but the quality of friendship has remained the same. About five years ago, I told a friend who lived across the country and was visiting town that we were lucky if we got to see each other once a year. Now with the demands of family life, I've revised that to feeling lucky to be able to talk on the phone a few times a year! However, given that the quality of the relationship isn't affected, there's nothing better than getting together with an old friend whom I haven't seen in years and picking up exactly where we left off!"

Speaking of her friend Diane, Marlene, a psychotherapist, says, "It's fascinating because we have led almost parallel lives. Five years would go by and we wouldn't have contact, and then we'll get back in touch and we've both taken the same life steps. We both became therapists at the same time, and we both lost children at the same time. One time I accidentally ran into her after a period of time, and, to our surprise, found out we were driving exactly the same car—green Peugeot 404 station wagons! Now we get together about once a year and take a walk, and we're always in the same place—you know, coming to terms with our creativity or our energy or where it's going."

Nina smiles when she describes a friendship she counts on, regardless of how much time has lapsed between contacts. She said, "One of my closest friends lives in Pittsburgh. I hadn't talked with her for nearly six months because she was studying for her board exams and she was out of commission. When I called, it was like I'd just talked with her last week."

Relaxed, secure, knowing the other understands our silences—these are the friendships that make us feel accepted, with no expectation to perform or be obligated to each other. Picking up where we left off is fine, and when we do so, we feel thoroughly nourished.

Helping Us Change
(Even When We'd Rather Not)

To act the part of a true friend requires more conscientious feeling than to fill with credit and complacency any other station or capacity in social life.

—SARAH ELLIS (1834)

Sometimes our friends recognize it is time for us to be in transition before we do. True friends help us grow, even when we'd prefer to stay right where we are. Lynn told us that a friend helped her to find her voice again, literally, after injury and malice had caused her to lose it. She had been a voice major in college, when she came under the unscrupulous tutelage of a teacher who was secretly jealous of the young women she taught. Following this voice teacher's malicious instructions, Lynn developed nodules on her vocal cords and could no longer sing. Lynn told us, "For years, I wouldn't sing at all. Nothing. The music had gone out of me. Debby, one of my lifelong friends, took it upon herself to get me to sing, but she knew me well enough to know that I can be quite a stubborn woman. So she tricked me. We'd be driving in her car, and she'd start singing a simple song like 'Jesus Loves Me,' and before long I'd be singing along with her. Then she'd sing a more difficult song, and without my realizing it, I'd sing that one, too. After a while, I was singing up a storm! She knew me so well that she knew I needed to get my voice back and that she'd have to be clever in how she helped me. Now that's a real friend!"

Deciding when to push a friend and when to hold back can be complicated, and all a woman can do is use her unique knowledge of that friend to make the decision. Sandra, a teacher, told this story of when her friend Ellen was in a violent relationship: "Ellen said that her other friends were just saying, 'Get out of there!' which was exactly my gut reaction. However, I said to her things like, 'I'm sure you would, if you could,' 'I see you laying your stepping stones.' I realized I had to put trust in her and help her have trust and confidence in her own process. I began to see and reflect for her that she was taking steps and that she had some kind of a trustworthy process.

"She did get out, and I felt I offered a different voice than other people who also really cared about her and were also perfectly right in being blunt. It's a tricky business knowing when you say it all and when you don't. Because that's the risk—you don't know. You don't know whether you haven't shown enough courage if you don't say it all, you don't know if you're not going to help by not saying it all. Very subtle."

Caring enough to get your hands dirty, even when you aren't asked for help, is the sign of a genuine friend. We might want our friends to leave us to our old ways, but these are the friends we need most when we get stuck. Dinah Shore wisely said, "Trouble is a part of your life, and if you don't share it, you don't give the person who loves you enough chance to love you enough."[19]

Vacations (The Minitransitions)

"The trouble is," said Laura, "walking in Venice becomes compulsive once you start. Just over the next bridge, you say, and then the next one beckons."

—DAPHNE DU MAURIER

Nobody ought to be too old to improve; I should be sorry if I was; and I flatter myself I have already improved considerably by my travels. . . .

—ANNE LETITIA BARBAULD (1785)

Some transitions change the direction of the rest of our lives. Others head us, temporarily, into a new geographical direction. These are commonly referred to as vacations. Traveling with a friend can be glorious; it may also be one of the most challenging experiences of your friendship. On the one hand, nothing is so rewarding as successfully following directions in another language (which neither of you speak very well, or at all) or viewing the Grand Canyon together for the first time or finding a restaurant that's not in a guidebook, complete with delicious local fare and an absence of other tourists. Nothing can bond you with your friend like escaping a scary-looking man who seems to be following you or the hilarity of watching American men gawk at topless women on a French beach.

On the other hand, traveling with a friend implies that you will become roommates, at least temporarily. Not only will you learn every idiosyncrasy of your friend's toilette, you will likely become intimately familiar with the state of her bowels and she with yours. You will learn more things about her and about your relationship than you ever thought possible. Some of these things will be niggling and annoying; random thoughts of ditching her in a gas station may come up. More than likely, however, you will become better friends for having lived through it; you will know each other better, have a greater abundance of embarrassing recollections with which to tease each other, and generally have stored away a unique basket of memories.

Learning just how long to spend with a particular friend on vacation can be an invaluable lesson. As Nina explained, "I have a friend who goes through extreme emotional swings where she's very up or very depressed. She's all over the page. I decided to take a vacation with her, knowing that I could hit her on a bad week. If the vacation landed on a bad week, I knew it would be horrible. And yet I took the risk, hoping for the 'up.'

"We rented a cottage on the beach, and it turned out to be a nice time. But the whole week I was anxious, anticipating when she was going to crash. I came home telling myself that this wasn't a great way to take a vacation.

"Last year I learned from my mistake and spent one night with her. She was very depressed, and I was quite glad I had to deal with her for only one night."

Carla, a painter in her midforties, summed up traveling with friends this way: "It's either great or awful, and there's nothing in between. It's really comfortable and really enlivening, it gives the trip a whole new dimension than it would have otherwise, or it's irritating. These extremes can happen with the same person, depending on what stage of our lives we're in and what's going on. When it's awful I think it has to do with exaggerated expectations, which I think come up periodically with girlfriends. So much of the time my connection with them is so rewarding and relatively effortless that I think I unconsciously fall into the expectation that it should always be that way. Then when it's not, trouble arises."

No matter how much fun you are having, difficulties will always arise when traveling in strange surroundings. Chris was traveling with her friend Jean in Europe after they had taken a bar exam to obtain their law licenses. She told us, "We had saved our money and planned this two-month trip to Europe. We rented a car and were completely carefree for what seemed an unbelievable expanse of time—no schedules, no requirements. We just traveled wherever we wanted to and stayed in places for however long fancied us. It was late summer, every place seemed more beautiful and intriguing than the last, and it seemed the world was our oyster. There will always be this golden glow around that period of time in my memory.

"Then, toward the end of the trip, we had the most awful moment in Florence. We got into this little traffic roundabout, and for some reason, every time we came to an exit off the roundabout, some policeman would wave us on. So we kept going around and around, and finally we just went off on this little alleyway, which got narrower and narrower. We approached a van, which we could just squeeze by. I don't know if I panicked or what happened, but all of a sudden I heard this horrible ripping sound; it was the worst sound I have ever heard. This metal step that we didn't see jutted out from underneath the van, and it cut a hole from the front tire of our car through the body to the back tire, like a can opener.

"So we were stuck. The alley was blocked off by a bunch of mopeds parked in front of us, so we couldn't go anywhere. Jean also noticed that we ripped the mirror off this van somehow. I didn't think the car was even high enough. So we were just terrified, picturing being stuck in some jail somewhere, trying to figure out how we were going to get out of this, and people screaming at us. The adrenaline kicked in, and Jean got out of the car. I could not believe my eyes: she picked the mopeds up—she didn't roll them, she picked them up—and moved them to the side so we could get through. And we took off!

"When we got back to Paris where we were supposed to drop the car off, I moaned, 'I am too embarrassed to explain this to the rental car clerk,' so Jean, bless her, said 'Okay, I'll take the paperwork in.' I know that was a sacrifice to her because we normally were both such rule followers. She said to the woman, 'We had a little bit of an accident.' And the woman asked, 'Did you have the insurance?' 'Yes,' said Jean. 'No problem,' the clerk replied, 'drive the car into the garage.' So we did. And we never heard anything more about it. But I will never forget how grateful I was to Jean for sparing me disgrace."

Most women (if enough time has passed) laugh when they think of their traveling disasters. Peg, a thirty-six-year-old freelance writer, traveled through Europe with her friend Kathy: "I took a trip with my high school best friend, and unfortunately, she was nauseated through the whole trip. I have pictures of her throwing up at all the landmarks in Paris, and when we got back, I put all of these pictures into a binder for her and titled it 'Kathy's Movable Feast.'"

When we travel with a friend, we share a universe with her. Every other thing fades away, and we become concerned, as a team, about the basic needs in life—where to eat, where to sleep, where to park the car, where to find a restroom, what to do for fun that day, where to find that "I love NY" thermometer for the collection. Concerns about what is going on at the job or the fight with a neighbor lose their importance. Isn't that what vacation is all about?

I Like Them Even When
They're Successful

The worst part of success is to try to find someone who is happy for you.

— BETTE MIDLER

Jealousy is all the fun you think they had.

— ERICA JONG

Inevitably, one friend may have more luck in money or love than the other. If one is succeeding and the other one isn't, a friendship may be tested, or it may raise certain barriers. Joanne, an author, spoke of being friends with another author: "I've been aware of competitive feelings coming up in relation to writing. My friend had just had a book published, and I had had a short story accepted by a magazine. She and I were both saying how great it was that we were both succeeding at the same time. I was getting ready to go to her book signing for her new book when I opened a horrendous letter saying the magazine had folded and my story wouldn't be printed. I was heartsick.

"Normally this is the friend that would have comforted me through such a loss, but here we all were celebrating her big, beautiful day. I walked into the book signing and told myself, 'You've got to squash what's going on for you to celebrate this thing of hers.' I was doing it for her, yet at the same time, I felt so dishonest when she said, 'Well, this time we really can celebrate together.' It's not an ongoing competitiveness, but there's a feeling of really wanting to be there for that person's big moment, even though you're dying inside. It's difficult."

Laura, a lawyer turned theatrical producer, was surprised by how few of her friends were able to share her early success. She said, "Shortly after I left my law practice, I produced a Broadway play, and was nominated for a Tony Award. All of these great things were happening to me, and all of a sudden, many of my friends didn't want anything to do with me. A couple of friends were right there with me, but many, many of my friends didn't talk to me, wouldn't call me. I guess they just couldn't deal with the fact that I had escaped a sort of unhappy life at the law firm. It's odd; I tried to win them back by telling them all the negative things I could think of about my life, like it isn't all that glamorous and I'm not making any money, that times are tough. It had no effect at all. The better things got, the more they just couldn't hear it. For a time this really dramatically reduced the number of friends that I had. I have a small group of friends who have survived the test, but relatively few.

"I was talking to a new friend of mine who was producing a successful play, and I mentioned my concern. She told me she'd always thought your true friends were revealed by what happens when times are tough, but her experience later proved that you could tell your true friends by your experience when times are really good for you."

No matter how apparently successful someone becomes, she still needs her friends. Success, too, is a transition, and a woman experiencing it may need her friends as much or more as when she seems beset with problems. What is success if we can't share it with our girlfriends?

Where Did She Go?

Where you used to be, there is a hole in the world,
which I find myself constantly walking around in the daytime,
and falling into at night.

—EDNA ST. VINCENT MILLAY

People change and forget to tell each other.

—LILLIAN HELLMAN

Sometimes, when our life takes a sharply different path from that of our friend, it feels like the person we knew is gone. But the friend we once knew is probably still there, and the past we had together is still a part of who she is. That shared world may be hidden for a while as her time is taken up with other matters, or it may take a change of scenery to see it. Linda, a business woman in her late thirties, tells this story: "My friend from college that I went to Europe with is now married, with a husband and kids and all that implies. We had had a very close emotional friendship when we were traveling together; we spent hours sleeping on trains together, going to museums together, and discussing intellectual matters. But when I was visiting at her house with her kids, I don't know what happened, we wouldn't talk about anything emotional or her plans or desires or any matters of the mind. It was really bizarre, because now I saw her as this suburbanite housewife, and she was very happy in that role. I thought, 'What happened to my friend Laura, the art history major, who walked through Notre Dame and so on?' I couldn't fit all of the pieces together.

"When we went off together on our own and started talking of the times we'd spent together, then it all came back. We went to a professional program together and went to a nice lunch afterward by ourselves, and that was a way we reconnected."

Another woman, now in her forties, had a similar story: "The relationship that I have with an old friend who at one time I was immensely close to has become sort of symbolic, in the sense that there's not a lot of depth to it anymore. All she ever talks about is either her personal life or other people's personal lives, and you can never have a conversation with her about ideas; conversation doesn't swing out to the intellectual and then swing back in to the personal, which I realize I really like. I've known her for twenty-five years, and she's really the one who followed the classic trajectory of being brilliant in college, brilliant in graduate school. Now all that's real to her are her kids and her disappointment in her divorce and her disappointment in her husband. As I talk to her, I'm thinking, 'Where did she go? What happened?'

"Recently, she and I and another friend went back to our college for a reunion. We had originally met there on the first day of school. The college is out in the country, and it's really different from where we are now—very green and humid and totally different from California. It's overwhelming, actually; the countryside kind of hits you in the face, and the fireflies and old houses and the crickets. We basically went back in time and rode everywhere on our rented bicycles, smoked dope, and acted like it was the late sixties and early seventies.

"We seemed to travel back in time, and for four days I felt about her the way I always used to; I felt completely in sync with her. We were all staying in the same bed and breakfast, we ate together, we went to all these events together. We had recreated the dorm experience, and it was wonderful. When we came back here, I realized there was no way to continue that feeling now that we were back in our real adult lives. That feeling still existed like a little enclosed world, and it's fascinating that it was possible to reenter it, given the correct circumstances, but not possible to bring it forward.

"Lately, I've felt like I just need to accept who she really is. This is who she turned out to be. I can't keep asking myself, 'What happened to the brilliant, fascinating woman that I knew when we went to graduate school together?' I have to recognize that if I am going to be friends with her now, I have to be friends with who she is now. I've been very sad at different times, I've been very annoyed with her at different times, but I need to figure out how to live with what is and stop struggling."

Our women friends are so much a part of who we are that when they no longer reflect us, we cannot easily accept it. We obviously do not have control over our friends' priorities, nor do they control our decisions. The woman above has provided her own wisdom: she must learn to accept what is and remember what part of her development she shares with her friend. The best we can do is hang on, learn in what ways we can be friends, and stay available. Perhaps our lives will wind around until they are in sync again.

The Test of Time

The growth of true friendship may be a lifelong affair.

—SARAH ORNE JEWETT (c. 1885)

Some friendships last, no matter what changes each party makes. This durability seems to come from the shared ability to mature and to be interested in growing as individuals. Arlene talks about how her friendship with Ellie has lasted through periods of great personal trauma for each of them, as well as through the shifting of attitudes and perceptions about themselves as people: "Our friendship spanned twenty-five years. Part of our relationship was based in a period of time when we were each trying to individuate from our husbands, who were very well known in their communities and in their respective industries. We were very supportive of each other. She introduced me to meditation, and we got more involved in the process of developing our spiritual natures. She and her family ended up moving close to where I lived, and we did a lot of inner exploration together, going on these spiritual journeys together. Then things got better in both of our lives.

"Oddly, if you're there to support somebody in their neurosis or in their crisis, the friendship may not make the transition when things get better. But we've been able to shift into different gears all the way along the life of our friendship."

Asked why she thought this was so, Arlene replied, "Well, I think that our basic ways of looking at the world are of interest to each other. And there was enough parallel experience that there was a good foundation. When her son was killed in an accident several years ago, she knew I had been through the experience of losing my son. I could be a resource for her, be there for her in ways that a lot of people couldn't. And so that was a very valuable time. There was something very important that I had to give.

"When she came out of that grief, we started discussing this idea in which we both had always been interested: 'How do you give form to the creative process?' This gave us direction, because we've always felt out of step with others around us. Her husband is a larger-than-life character, and my husband created his business from scratch and has always been very focused. Ellie's and my minds didn't move that way. Ellie and I had nonlinear lives, and there was no single direction in our work."

Friendships, like the one between Arlene and Ellie, survive for two reasons. One is that the friends share enough similarity in experience that they can identify and empathize with the other. The far more important reason however—the absence of which destroys many relationships—is the desire and ability to grow and stretch with each other in mutual development as human beings. When we make room for each other to mature, change, explore, and experiment, we make room for friendship that can stand the tests of time.

Remembering Friends

Of course you can go home again!
You just look in your heart for your old best friend!

—HELEN MOSS

Friendships have their own life cycles. They can continue to evolve, adapting through changes in our circumstances and lives. We honor these adaptive friends in various ways, at birthday time or other events over a lifetime. Unfortunately, a life cycle implies that friendships can also die. They may come to a sudden or gradual halt through a disagreement or through a change in life too big or too frightening for the friendship to stretch and adapt to fit to the change. And sadly, the nature of human existence means that we sometimes lose our friends through illness and death.

Because our friendships help shape us in a myriad of ways, we take our girlfriends with us long after we can no longer hear their voices or see their smiles. By remembering our girlfriends we satisfy the longing penned by English poet Amelia Opie in 1802: "But thou mayest grant this humble prayer, / Forget me not! forget me not!"[20]

Celebrating Birthdays

And many more . . .

What is celebrating a birthday without our friends? We need our girlfriends to share so many aspects of our special day. Pat told us, "I am grateful that Carmen helps me have birthday parties. We didn't do birthday parties in my family, so celebrating my birthday as an adult has always been hard for me. I appreciate her patience over the years, helping me celebrate to the point I could handle. At first, she'd have parties for just the two of us. Then, when I turned thirty-five, she helped me throw a party at my house, and we invited other people. This year, for my fortieth, I threw a big bash at the racetrack, inviting lots of people. Carmen helped with the invitation and other things. But most of all, she helped me learn how to celebrate myself and allow people to show affection for me."

Friends can also hold our memories for us and reflect back to us things about ourselves and our lives that we had buried in some inaccessible place in our minds. Joanne, in her fifties, gives this example: "Some years ago a friend of mine from college was turning fifty, and her daughter sent out a letter to a number of her mother's friends, asking if her friends would have anything to contribute to a book of pictures and memories of her mother's past.

"I sat down and wrote my recollection of this friend and me in the south of France together as students and our various adventures, like taking off and spending the night somewhere without having baggage. I had a delightful time writing this account. The daughter wrote back and said, 'This is so fabulous, we're going to open the book with it.'

"When my friend got it, she said, 'This is one of the wonderful things about friendships that go way, way back, because you fill in the details.' Some things that I had written she had forgotten, and in turn the friends who are my age, who go way back, fill in details for me. We remember things when the other one has forgotten them, and then it's like giving each other something back, and that is just wonderful."

Even though Katherine and Leslie are grown women, they still love to celebrate their birthdays like playful little girls. Katherine described a celebration for Leslie: "We met on the beach for her birthday. I knew she wanted lots of ribbon and balloons and stuff. So I got a bag full of little gifts wrapped up, and we had lunch on a bench. We both wore hats and dresses. It was fun, sitting there like little girls eating our sandwiches!"

The birthday girl is usually the one who receives the gifts. But sometimes we receive a great deal when celebrating someone else's birthday, as illustrated by Claudette. Claudette describes her best friend, Nancy, as a strong woman who has survived some tragic events. Claudette has learned not only about strength from her friend, but also about play and celebration. She told us, "For Nancy's fiftieth birthday party, we made her house into a journey with Alice in Wonderland, including an underground rabbit's tunnel with roots painted on reams of crumpled paper covering the entire stairway from her garage to her foyer and up into the house. During this play time, I was the only person who could do parts of the artwork, according to her. This was just one of the times she flattered me into using my talents to the fullest."

Birthdays are a way to find out we have affected people in ways we never knew. Esther, a fifty-five-year-old photographer, illustrates with this story: "For my fiftieth birthday, two of my good friends got together and decided to give me a surprise party, but they didn't really know who a lot of my friends were. So they invited people that they somehow associated with me, and a lot of them were from the past, not my current friends. As a result, the guests around the table constituted my history, and everybody told a story about how I had affected that person's life or how we had met. It was like the eulogies that you get when you die, except that I got them when I was alive. It was the most wonderful gift, because we say things sometimes that we don't necessarily remember, but may provide the guiding light that takes someone to the next step in their lives. I heard about the influence that I had had on people's lives of which I was totally unaware. It was an enormous gift."

Birthdays are a great opportunity to celebrate our girlfriends, regardless of who the birthday girl is. It doesn't have to be an expensive production, just an occasion or a gift that makes our girlfriend understand that a gaping hole would exist in our lives if she had never been born. Go ahead and embarrass her; let her know how important she is—with witnesses, too. When we are the birthday girl, we have carte blanche to do whatever we want, including telling our friends how valuable they are, no matter how much they wiggle and squirm and try to deflect the compliment. Birthdays are the perfect excuse to say the affectionate things we feel, but somehow never get around to saying.

Losing Touch

For we lose not only by death, but also by leaving and being left, by changing and letting go and moving on.

—JUDITH VIORST

There is a bond nothing can ever loosen.
What I have lost: what I possess forever.

—RACHEL

Ours is a mobile society, and it is easy to lose track of friends who used to be important parts of our daily lives. It seems odd to think that we can go for years without talking to a person with whom we had regular contact. It is even odder when we realize we have no idea how to reach someone. Linda, a San Francisco attorney, told us the story of her frustration of trying to track down a childhood friend:

181

"I haven't been able to find my best girlfriend from seventh grade, Ann. We used to play the guitar together, and Herman's Hermits and Simon and Garfunkel were our favorite groups. I got this phone call from her out of the blue, saying, 'Linda, I haven't talked to you for years, but I found your number. I'm moving from Vermont, so give me a call if you want to get back in touch.' This was when I was on vacation, and I didn't get back until two weeks later. So I called the number she left, and a recording said, 'We have no forwarding number.' She had already moved! It was so frustrating, I almost hired a detective just to find her. She and her husband taught at a school in Vermont. I ripped through everything looking for her old address, but I couldn't find it. I sent a letter to the telephone company, even, saying, 'Please forward this to her.' I was desperate to find her. Finally, I got a list of schools and called the one where I thought they had been employed. They did have the address of where she moved. They wouldn't give it to me, but I sent them a letter a few weeks ago and they are going to forward it to her."

How frustrating it is to have lost a friend and then not be able to find her. To avoid the frustration, we may try to check in with our friends occasionally. If there is someone in our address book we haven't communicated with in years or an old friend we have been thinking about lately, maybe we should try to find her. Sometimes it doesn't take very much—calling her family members or directory assistance. When we reach her, we may find that our rediscovered friend says something like "I was just thinking of you" or "I can't believe that you called, I was just talking about you." Those we hold dear can sometimes share our thought tracks, and times may come when we are thinking of each other simultaneously. So when these "random thoughts" come up, we may need to track down our friend. If she cannot be found, we needn't despair. Remember there are only six degrees of separation from every other person in the world, and we will probably cross paths with her again.

Reaching Our Limits

You know when you have your answering machine turned on because you're afraid your friend is going to call, something is wrong with the friendship.

—KATHLEEN BYRNE

All healthy friendships operate within boundaries mutually agreed upon by both parties. Occasionally, one friend will find it necessary to set limits for herself that may feel uncomfortable, or even painful to the other. At times it's important to be honest and say "This is as far as I can go. I've reached my limit." Sometimes we enter a relationship that we soon see is an unhealthy one—we began the friendship with mutuality, but discover our friend really needs professional help. We quickly find that they expect us to support them emotionally, but—here's the key—we don't receive the same kind of support from them.

Twenty-two-year-old Jennifer expressed feeling "sucked dry" by a friend: "In high school I had this friend who was thoroughly messed up, but in high school you're not going to suggest to your friends that they try a support group. That's a sign of weakness, and you don't deal with that kind of stuff in high school. So I took on a lot of her problems and began feeling like I was solely responsible for her happiness and well being. She knew I was willing to give her a lot and began taking advantage of it. There were times when I was at her house constantly, and then she'd make a switch all of a sudden and not want to talk to me. It got to the point where I knew I couldn't deal with it anymore; I felt totally sucked dry. We never talked about me, we only talked about the boy of the week that she was seeing or this and that, and my needs were totally ignored.

"I finally ended the friendship and I haven't talked to her in years now. After we went to college, she tried to get back in contact with me. She wrote me this letter saying, 'Oh, you were the best friend I ever had' and all this stuff, and I just felt, 'I can't go back to that,' because I knew that she hadn't started dealing with those issues. I wrote her back and said, 'I'm sorry, I just don't have room in my life to take care of you,' because I knew I couldn't do it. That was really hard, but it was almost a relief. After I finally said, 'No more,' it was like a weight was lifted off of my shoulders. It was so much healthier for me to get out of the relationship."

Kathleen, a forty-six-year-old writer, talked about her response when she feels that she is not getting anything from a relationship: "If I'm having that feeling that someone is always needy, always depressed, and they're not turning to other resources, I try not to just fade away from her. I think that is really cruel, so I say, 'You know, I feel like your problem is so great that I can't help you. Have you thought of going to a therapist or a women's group or a rabbi or a twelve-step group or someone? I love you, but I really can't hear this again about George or about your weight,' or whatever. You can be a real friend, I think, by being honest in that situation."

Another type of limit is reached if we experience an unexpected termination of a friendship—a friend suddenly pulls away without explanation. An unexplained ending is probably more about the person ending it than the person being abandoned. Perhaps she cannot face conflict, and saying what prompted the ending would be too much for her to bear. Nevertheless, the experience is still painful. Sandra, a teacher, suffered the ending of a treasured friendship and still does not know why her friend cut her off. Sandra told us, "We lived in different places, and I would visit her when I was in her town. Then she sent me a little note saying she didn't want to see me anymore. It was a shock to me. I telephoned her and I said, 'You know, it seems to me there's probably more to this.' There was this long, terrible silence, and then she denied it. I wrote her a note and said I was really sorry for whatever I might have done that hurt her or made her angry or whatever it was, and it was very frustrating to me that I had to deal with that totally one-sidedly. But she wouldn't talk about it. That was very hard for me, because I'm somebody who wants to work things through with people. It turned out there was a real limitation to that friendship."

Our healthy friendships have room in them for one of us to be more needy at times than the other, and for one of us to set boundaries for ourselves. Friendships can break off if both parties are not willing to recognize boundaries or eventually engage in a balanced give and take. If boundaries can never be respected by one of us, as in Jennifer's story, or one of us is always the needy one, never able to offer help to the other, as in Kathleen's example, the relationship is not a healthy one for either one of the friends.

A healthy relationship also can contain and respect fear—fear of being angry or fear of a friend's illness or trouble. Fear may be overcome if a person obtains the help she needs or musters up the courage to face whatever goblins haunt her. But we may feel frustrated or helpless if we watch a friend back away out of fear or even if we are the one backing away in fear, unable to speak of it. If one of us has reached her limit, all the other can really do is offer encouragement, and let her know that she is loved. With time, help, and courage, we may each be able to offer our hearts (and voices) up fully.

Between Friends

Everything in life that we really accept undergoes a change.

—KATHERINE MANSFIELD

There are times in life when we are between friends—we have moved, begun another phase in our life, or gotten divorced and lost some of our friends. In these periods of transition, we realize who are those friends that we will carry forward and which ones will be merely a memory, a facet of a certain period of our life. Sometimes that realization is painful, as when you realize that the woman who was married to your ex-husband's best friend was actually a friend of convenience, that you were "couple friends" but nothing more. These kind of relationships are valid, but the realization can be painful if two people had different expectations about their friendship.

Sometimes when we have made a transition, we have to go looking for new friends or wait for them to find us. Nineteen-year-old Erica, who just moved across the country to go to college, is searching for a new friend: "Having just left my high school friends, but not yet having developed good friendships at college, I feel kind of stuck in the middle. I am still in contact with my high school buddies, but it's hard to communicate when we're two thousand miles apart. I want to meet people here, but I have found it difficult to find self-respecting girls who know how to think and have fun. I guess I am looking for a very rare kind of friendship, and I will have to be patient. There definitely is a very unique bond that forms between females, and it takes time to develop." In times of transition, confidence and patience will help us find the right friends for us.

Sometimes in life there just doesn't seem to be time to have friends. Holly, a mother of two starting her own apparel business, writes, "I've had many close and loving relationships with women over the years. The 'inseparable' friends of my high school days have fallen away. I was the first to get married, and the priorities for my life changed. My connection with my husband was a pretty closed involvement. Because of that deep connection, I didn't miss my women friends. After the birth of our son John, I began playing tennis. That fall, I began my first indoor tennis season. Suddenly, I was surrounded by women."

So, we must take heart when life changes, or we are feeling friendless. The same currents that led us away from old friends will lead us to new ones. Perhaps an unknown agent will lead us to her door. Lida, a songwriter, tells this story, "Jinny and I met through our youngest children. My doorbell rang one morning, and I opened the door to find the skinniest, red-haired, freckled-faced, runny-nosed kid I'd ever seen. He wanted to know if he could play with 'that girl'—'that girl' being my three-year-old blond, freckle-faced, runny-nosed Gia. I figured that since they obviously had a great deal in common already and since we'd just moved into the neighborhood, I'd better find out where this boy lived and meet his mother!

"He very obligingly escorted us to a house two lots up the street, walked into his kitchen, and shouted something like, 'I've brought that girl home!' The woman who came in response to his shout was certainly his mother! Tall, red-haired, freckled and slim, although, unlike her son, she didn't have a tendency to wipe her nose on her sleeve. I was somewhat apprehensive about the mothering skills of a woman who'd let a three year old go down the street to total strangers, but after her warm and gracious welcome, I realized Jinny didn't know any 'strangers,' and neither did her son!"

They are out there waiting, all kinds of wonderful women who may be the next stars in our universe of friends. All we need is faith that they will show themselves when we are ready for them. Haven't they always?

Lake Ladies

Yes'm, old friends is always best, 'less you can catch a new one that's fit to make an old one out of.

—SARAH ORNE JEWETT (1896)

Many of us do not live the traditional life of being married and/or having children. The women born of and after the baby boomer generation seem especially to lead lives that do not conform to traditional roles of wife and mother. The authors count themselves among that group. In our middle thirties and early forties and both unmarried, we have each developed a network of friends who have become our families, to whom we are committed. Each of us has a friend with whom we check in almost daily; each of us discusses with our friends the big and little decisions we must make. We share intimate information about ourselves—even the most intimate of all, our bank account balances—and discuss how we should work out the issues in our lives.

These friends are one of the few constants in our lives—the women who are there if we find out that a boyfriend has been having an affair with someone else, if we are fired from a job, if our doctor tells us the PAP smear was a "little funny" and she wants to do some more tests. As we get older without having found a mate (that, of course, could fill several other books) or deciding that we are better off without one (yet more books), these relationships become even more indispensable. These are the friends who know our whole history.

When we spoke with Stephanie Salter, a columnist for the *San Francisco Examiner*, about our project, she told us about the Lake Ladies, a group of childhood friends who continue, every year, to meet at a lake cabin where they played as children. Stephanie referred us to her column of April 25, 1989, part of which we decided to share with you:

We call ourselves the Lake Ladies because for years now we've traveled back to our Indiana homeland during the same summer week to renew the bonds of friendship in a vacation house on a little manmade lake.

For four of us the A-frame house dates back to deepest darkest junior high school when we were sullen little sacks of howling hormones and the adults in charge were my friend Marilyn's parents.

Throughout high school and college we practiced a variety of skills at the lake: water skiing, cussing, making and drinking martinis, imitating Diana Ross and the Supremes, restructuring foreign policy and falling in love.

Now . . . we are the adults in charge. Loosely speaking.

. . . Probably the most distinctive characteristic of the Lake Ladies—other than our just getting together all the time—is our collective singleness. Among the gang of six there has been but one marriage (long kaput) and nary a child.

None of us set out to live this solitary life, I think. No Dickensian childhoods haunt us. In fact, all of the Lake

Ladies come from the kind of traditional, nuclear family that Ronald Reagan and George Bush believe will save America.

Like many men and women of our postwar generation, we just sort of evolved into "Unmarried — Without Children," a state that still inspires outright insult ("Aw, no husband?") or subtle cracks about "people who refuse to grow up."

Hey, we've grown up, we just haven't done it the way traditionalists insist you must. We believe you can be a grown-up and continue to imitate the Supremes.

Happily, the Lake Ladies have each other in their odd-ness and . . . [t]he older we grow, the stronger the bonds of our extended family become. . . . So, naturally, when the subject of Marilyn and Helen's impending birthdays sur-faced this past summer, we all agreed we had to be in the same place for the first Big Four-O's to come down.

We were headed by separate airlines for centrally located Denver. Marilyn, who lives there, had rented a video camera, reserved a limousine and a table at a fancy restaurant up in the Rockies where the actual birthday din-ner was to take place. We also were scheduled to go out dancing and learn the Texas two-step. The odds are excel-lent that we also played at least one grumbling round of Trivial Pursuit.

The odds are equally excellent that on departure day we stood en masse at Stapleton Airport, hugging and weeping as if we were all shipping out for active duty in the Pacific. The Lake Ladies cry a lot when they say good-bye.

We do this because we love each other, because we secretly fear each time could be the last time and because — after all these years — the whole Lake Ladies phenomenon still seems too good to be true.

I mean, anything that looks as though it will be as fun in menopause as it was puberty, is my idea of a successful institution.[21]

That column was written in 1989. When we interviewed Stephanie recently, it appeared that the Lake Ladies institution was as strong as ever. The Lake Ladies now own the cabin together. And the one Lake Lady who married in the interim came to an understanding before taking the vows that she would still take this vacation with the Lake Ladies every year.

When the Lake Ladies met for their forty-fifth birthday celebration, they videotaped themselves watching the videotape of their fortieth celebration. "We all sat around and laughed and taped ourselves laughing and watching the videotape, so that we could all individually go home and laugh at the videotape of ourselves laughing at the videotape!" Her description recalls the image of standing between two mirrors. Looking into one of the mirrors, many layers of reflections are revealed, an infinite number of images. Lifelong friends keep reflecting one another endlessly — back and forth, layer upon layer.

Wishing for More

I believe that what woman resents is not so much giving herself in pieces as giving herself purposelessly.

—ANNE MORROW LINDBERGH

Some women told us that, as they thought back on their friendships, they wished for something different or something more—more guidance, more honesty, more support, more kindness. When we acknowledge how important other women are in our lives, we also open up the possibility of disappointment.

KC, a woman who had endured an abusive marriage for several years before finally getting out, said that she felt her closest girlfriends failed her in one respect. She had needed more truth telling from women to help her out of a life-threatening situation. She told us, "I finally left the marriage, and, believe me, it took me a long time to do that. A lot of my very good friends came to me and said, 'I'm glad you left. You know, you should have left a long time ago,' or 'We always thought he was a terrible person.' Nobody ever said that to me when I was in the marriage. No one helped me see just how bad it really was.

"The truth is, it took me a long time because I had to build up my confidence all by myself. I was building my steps to leave, and I think if someone had even recognized that, I would have felt validated and stronger. As it was, I felt invisible through the marriage, and I felt invisible after the marriage. The moment I left seemed to redefine the past six years, and somehow it was wrong and all my fault. I was thinking, 'Wait a minute, I dealt with it in the way I could, and no one said anything before.'"

Marion, now a counselor, also expressed disappointment in the way that a group of women she had believed were her friends responded when she lost her job and began making personal changes. First, she felt unsupported during her time of grief and disorientation. She told us, "We all went out to lunch and there was a real strain. Finally, when everyone put her cards on the table, it was 'Well, you've changed. You've become more self-centered, and you're not reaching out to us like you used to.' I realized then that I had built this network of female friends that wasn't reciprocal.

"I had been there when they gave birth to their babies, I had been an incredibly codependent person, giving, giving, giving. But when it came to a needy time in my life, I felt judged for it. Not judged because I was needy, but because I was in too much pain to give to them. I didn't have any resources left. I cried all through that lunch.

"Later I got a letter from one of those women telling me basically what a selfish bitch I had become. That was a very painful time for me. For quite a while I didn't initiate any relationships with women. I poured myself into reading and reached out to men for friendship. Fortunately, there were other women friends who initiated contact, and I was able to trust women again."

These are painful memories. A friend may not always be there for us, and we may not always be there for a friend. It is up to each person to decide whether that disappointment is severe enough that the friendship is not worth pursuing or whether the disappointment can be worked through. Whatever we decide, we will have learned something about ourselves, and about which aspects of friendship are important to us. This knowledge can be used to improve our own friendship abilities as well as to be on the lookout for those women who really practice the friendship skills we value. Given human nature and circumstance, we are bound to disappoint occasionally or be disappointed. We need to take what we can from the experience, and be ready to forgive ourselves and others.

One Never Forgets

Memory is more indelible than ink.

—ANITA LOOS

Losing a friend through illness and death is heartbreaking, and the fact that we have no control over it is bewildering. Fern tells us her sad memory. "My friend Connie had a rare form of cancer, one about which no one, not even the experts, knew much. Our friendship deepened in efforts to find a way to prolong her life. Since we lived in a small town in the Midwest, I would take turns with her husband and other friends to drive the hundred miles to the nearest medical center that was able to treat her—sometimes once a week over a nine-year period. As these efforts failed to stem the cancer storming through her body, she and her husband started investigating a broader range of possible treatments, and they found a medical center in the West that was willing to try some experimental treatments on her. She and her husband drove out there and found her an apartment; the treatment plan was going to last several months. When the treatments were over, she needed someone to drive her back home; the treatments had left her weak and she did not feel able to drive all the way back to Illinois. Her husband, a CPA who was stuck in the middle of tax season, was under a lot of pressure at work, so I volunteered to drive her back from the San Francisco Bay Area, where she was located.

"We had planned to come straight home, but once I was there, it didn't really seem that was necessary. We both had a sense that Connie was not going to get any better, and we decided that perhaps we didn't have to hurry home after all. It became our 'Thelma and Louise' trip. We started out from San Francisco and drove down the coast to San Luis Obispo and saw the Hearst Castle. Then turning east, we headed toward Las Vegas. When we reached Las Vegas, we heard that storms were going to be passing through the area where we would be driving and decided that we would just spend some time in Vegas, gambling and going to shows. We had a marvelous time, just two Midwestern gals doing as we pleased. The whole time we did not directly talk of Connie's illness. She seemed not to want to do so, and she insisted on 'protecting' me from her disease. She always made sure her head was covered—she had lost all of her hair—and that I did not see how her illness had ravaged her body. We just shared the unspoken knowledge that she was going to die. After our few days in Las Vegas, we left and traveled over the rolling plains to our home. On our last day of driving, an angry, dark storm front followed us all across the plains, an all too literal reminder of the other deadly storm gaining on her. 'Just keep pushing down the pedal, Fern,' she kept saying, looking straight ahead. We pulled into her garage seconds before a huge thunderstorm broke. Connie did die, two years later. I miss her terribly still, and that was over ten years ago. But she does live in my memory, and I am reminded of her every time I look at her picture, which sits on my shelf."

Marilyn, a jewelry designer, recently lost a friend who both inspired and drew upon Marilyn's creativity. "My friend Merle Shain died, and it's strange because I sometimes dream about her. It's so hard to lose friends like that with whom you had so much shared life. We grew up in Toronto together. When I had a shop in Toronto—I was a designer of women's apparel and she bought marvelous things from me—we became very good friends. She was very visual also. Very self-absorbed, but also very generous. She was a very sweet woman."

Asked about their emotional connection, Marilyn replied, "I think it had to do with our creative lives. For her, I know what it was: I really lived on the edge in my twenties, with painters and all the rest of it, and she was intrigued by my choices. She was brought up in a strict Jewish background and my life seemed exotic in comparison. When she was older and divorced, she had the opportunity to explore, and my background and hers merged. Her intellectual and literary bent was my attraction to her. We had the best conversations. Long and very up in the air, a lot of fantasy. When it came to problem areas, Merle was more of a poet. Merle's reality was a special rich mix that intensely appealed to me. She had a great capacity for fun and adventure. The thing I think I miss most about her was that she took enormous delight in everything. Everything—flowers—she had a lovely garden, a beautiful house—people. Had a marvelous, giggly laugh, she was very quick to laugh. I do miss that. She was a real dear."

Perhaps we wonder what will happen to our friends' memories of us after we die. Some of us may worry that we will be forgotten, unimportant. But our friends do not forget. Like George Bailey learned in *It's a Wonderful Life*, we affect people in ways that we will never know. Lucy, now in her mideighties, talks of her best friend when she was six years old: "A family near us had many children. One day my favorite, age eight, came home with me to spend the night. She lived with us until her death at age eighteen. It was horrible to lose her. She had dark hair like my parents, and as a blond myself, some people thought I was the child who had come to live with the family. I still think of her."

When we examine sunlight streaming through a window, we notice the dust motes sparkling, moving, dancing in the air. So it is with our memories of our friends and their memories of us. We may not even know they are there, unless the full light of our consciousness comes to rest on a memory. But they are always present, dancing, moving, swirling in our thoughts and around and through our souls.

Baking Bread (For Camille)

by Laura Gilpin

Sunday, mid-afternoon, mid-December:
the sky wanting so badly to snow
that I feel like crying.
A good day, you tell me, for nothing
but baking bread
so I pack up the loaf pans, the recipe,
stop at the corner store
for flour, milk, two cakes of yeast.

All the way to your apartment
the wind gnaws like a hungry
animal begging at my feet.
But the light in your kitchen always
glows warmly. You lend me a sweater
and turn on the oven for heat
and we pull the chairs up close
as though the stove was an old woman
and we were children and she had just
offered us something good to eat.

After a while, I'm not cold anymore.
You have made tea in the Japanese pot
with a broken lid. I let the steam
rise into my hands, disappear through my fingers.
I want to tell you how grateful I am

but you have put on a record
and are singing harmony with Tammy Wynette.

We stand in your kitchen now
measuring, sifting:
12 cups of flour, 2 cups of milk,
half-cup of sugar, teaspoon of salt.
Such basic ingredients; we stir and knead.

Darkness arrives early
like a distant relative
with nowhere else to go.
We sit in the living room
waiting for the bread to rise.
I read on the sofa in the lamp's light
while you sing "Stand by Your Man"
with Loretta Lynn, sewing a hem
into the second-hand dress
you will, years from now,
wear to your wedding.

But neither of us knows that yet.
Neither of us knows that months from now
I will fall out of love with the man
I have been with for a long time
or that you will marry the man
you have just met.
Later, you will move, with your husband,
farther away. A distance

will grow between us,
but we don't know that yet.

Doubled in size, the dough rises
like a winter moon, pale and luminous.
Snow begins to sift down
softening the darkness.
The record ends but you keep singing,
breaking the thread with your teeth.

We shape the dough
into four small loaves, smooth and rounded
as though we might shape our lives with such care
Soon the kitchen will expand
with the fragrance of baking bread.
You will pour me another cup of tea.
I will try to find a way to say thank you,
try to explain how, for so long, I believed
everything I owned was borrowed,
that I had nothing I could call my own to give.

As I lift the first loaf from the oven
it will burn in my hands like an offering.
After we have made a meal of warm bread, butter and
     honey,
I will try to tell you once more how grateful I am
but you have put on the long white dress and are dancing.

Women's Rites

One evening I came home from a quilting bee —
where twelve women, ages twenty-two to eighty-five,
had sat around a large quilting frame, working,
chatting, and gossiping — to find seven women
gathered at Emma's kitchen table.
A party was underway . . . .

SUE BENDER

Plain and Simple:
A Woman's Journey to the Amish

Reasons to Rendezvous

Women have traditionally sought out other women, bene-
fiting from the enjoyment of one another's company. Even
when leisure time was nonexistent and home was the exclusive province of women's lives, women devised projects
that would bring them together—quilting bees, canning
vegetables, going to the marketplace to find food. While
we may no longer need to sew our own blankets for
warmth or can food in order to survive the winter, women
still need feminine companionship, and today's women
have devised a number of activities around which to gather.

Over the ages, women have shared rituals to honor
every aspect of life. Some of these rituals have been
modified, expanded, and incorporated into the fabric of
life's most cherished events: celebrating birthdays, finding
something old, blue, and new at a wedding, throwing a
baby shower, and picking out flowers for a funeral. In the
past, major life events were acknowledged in the community; marriages, births, funerals were all part of the social
order, acknowledging and marking the expected events in
life. For good or for ill, life in our Western society is not so
orderly, and a lot more goes on in women's lives today—
other passages to mark, acknowledge, celebrate.

We've collected ideas from women about their favorite girlfriend activities, and we've added some of our own favorites for celebrating friendships.

Birthdays

While we are officially celebrating our births, birthdays can draw our attention, sometimes against our will, to the aging process. Acknowledging that we've lived another year can be both joyful and painfully excruciating. Here are some of the ways the women we interviewed enhanced the traditional birthday celebration.

Have a professional photo taken with one or more of your special girlfriends to celebrate your birthdays. Rene and Carmen got all dolled up and had a professional photo shoot taken together the year they both turned forty "as a milestone for each of us individually and for our friendship."

Construct a theme birthday party for yourself or a friend that celebrates being a woman. Nina found a poem that she shared with the women she invited to her party. Linda asked her friends to bring something to read that contained some wisdom or feeling that her guest wanted to share with the birthday girl and other guests.

If you are a mother of a daughter, give her the gift of your friends' wisdom. Margaret celebrated her daughter's twenty-first birthday by gathering Margaret's own friends together, those women she felt had something in terms of wisdom, direction, or inspiration from their life experiences to share with her daughter. When her daughter is in times of conflict or difficulty, she can replay the tape of the party and hear these women, aged from forty to eighty, talk about the hurdles that they had overcome, the strengths and benefits they had gained, and what had inspired them in difficult times. Margaret's daughter received the sum total of over a dozen women's accumulated life experience to take with her into adulthood.

Marriage

When a friend marries, throw a teacup party. Each woman invited brings a different teacup and saucer, reflecting her own taste, all wrapped up. After the gifts are unwrapped, they are used for a tea party. The bride keeps the teacups as a way of commemorating the women in her life. Each teacup is different and reflects the personality of the giver, and she is reminded of each of her friends as she uses the cups in the future.

∾

Recognize your friends verbally at your own wedding. Kathleen told us about Elly's wedding, the first in her group of friends to get married, in which, "instead of going with the usual throwing-the-bouquet tradition, she made six separate beribboned bouquets and tossed them to us from a balcony, one by one, with sweet words, during her wedding reception." When Jackie married, she wrote each of her closest friends, telling each what she especially valued about her.

Babies

When a new baby is coming, one group of women we know gives the new mother a handmade quilt in which each member contributes a square. What a lovely gift for both mother and child!

Welcome the new mother home with a much-appreciated gift. Elizabeth told us that she throws a welcome-home dinner for the mother and her family when they return home from the hospital. Or organize with several friends to supply dinners for the family for two weeks.

Make a time capsule for the new baby. Ask each of the expectant mother's friends to bring an item that personifies the age in which the baby will be born. For an added twist, ask each friend to guess what she thinks the child will look like at age twenty-five, how tall he or she will be at that age, what line of work he or she will be pursuing, and so on. We heard of an African village tradition: when a new baby is on the way, the village gathers to speculate on why this child is being sent at this time, in this place: "What are we needing now that this child is sent to add among us?" The adults thus look at themselves and welcome the baby into that circle.

∾

Have a speakerphone baby shower. Connie was expecting twin boys, and the night before her friends were to throw a big co-ed baby shower, she was rushed to the hospital to stop a premature delivery. At first all were discouraged by the thought of calling off the festivities, and then someone came up with the great idea of having two showers at the same time, with some of the friends joining Connie at the hospital and the others at the home site with her husband, Trevor. Connie and Trevor communicated with each other and friends via the speakerphone, with Connie first opening one present and ooohing and aahhing and then Trevor opening another. So, if you can't get the shower to the mother or the mother to the shower, or if you can't get all of the expectant couple's friends in the same location, a speakerphone baby shower will provide an experience no one will forget!

Writing Connection

Keep those cards and letters coming! Most of us eagerly anticipate cards and photographs from friends who are far away. And it doesn't matter when we get them. Carolyn sends Easter cards, because that is when she finishes writing the cards she meant to send at Christmas.

Reconnect with a friend who has slipped away from regular contact by writing a letter to her, describing in detail one of your favorite memories of her.

Start your own creative writing workshop. Elise, Leslie, Sarah and Michele met each week to pick a random topic, wrote together for a set period of time (such as an hour), and then shared what they had written. If you are interested in developing your creative side, this is a great way to do it. So far, Leslie has gone on to publish a book!

Holidays

Holidays are a great time to continue or begin a private joke. Kathleen confessed that she and her friend, Maggie, have sent a plastic poinsettia back and forth with their Christmas gifts each year for the last fifteen years.

In the midst of holiday craziness, Cheryl carves out a bit of time each year to get together with her friends for glasses of champagne. "As we sit talking and laughing, I think, 'This is great! I just love sitting here, and am so happy to be with these people.'" What better time to take a few moments to appreciate your friends?

∾

On Independence Day, gather your friends together and have each woman declare herself independent of a specific fear or insecurity she has about herself.

∾

Plan now for New Year's Eve 1999. Who better to include in your celebrations for the next millennium than your best girlfriends?

Traditions

Create a tradition. Find something that you do every year (or more) with the same friend or friends. Carey plans a river rafting trip every year for her women friends, which she calls "Amazons Down the River." Go to a local restaurant for high tea. One group of friends is crazy about basketball; they see high school, college, and professional games whenever they can.

∾

Go to the spa together. Nobody but your girlfriend can appreciate the luxury of having a pedicure together. Or create your own spa. Two office mates told us, "Whenever we have a chance, which is a couple of times a week, we give each other back massages. It relieves the stress, and it's a ritual we share together."

Plan an adventure. Rene told us about a group of single, career women who take turns planning an adventure each month, known only to the woman who is planning it. The adventure has to cost less than twenty dollars per person, and all the other women are told is what to wear. One month it was hot air ballooning. Borrowing from *Fried Green Tomatoes*, their secret cry is "Tawanda!"

Go to the woods. Joanna and Kate love hiking and being out in the wilderness. "For both of us, the wilderness is a vital source of comfort and well being, and our trips always leave us feeling revitalized and at peace. We have been friends for so long that we are quite comfortable hiking along in companionable silence, although we also thoroughly enjoy arguing over wildflower identification." Some friends are happier doing some urban hiking, otherwise known as shopping. Pick whatever refreshes you.

If you have children, encourage them to talk about who their best friends are and why they like them so much. Start them off by telling what you appreciate most about one of your closest friends. Tape your story and send it to your friend. Not only will you be teaching your children to appreciate friendship, but your friend will always have a record of why you think she's wonderful.

Everyday Rituals

Some rituals may seem mundane on the surface, such as going shopping or sharing a cup of tea. But these womanly rites, whether grand or everyday, strengthen bonds of friendship and give us the courage and direction we need.

Make lunch a special occasion. Rene and her friend use their lunchtime as a regular friendship ritual. She said, "We often want to talk without a lot of distraction or interruption at work, so we opt for an alfresco lunch in our favorite park, sitting on a bench or blanket in the sunshine. To spend a few moments with my dear friend and with nature can be refreshing to the mind and spirit."

Have a cup of java. Women used to take a break by sharing coffee over a kitchen table. Some still do, but many may be more likely to go to the local coffee shop. Penny described, "Sometimes after a particularly trying day, we'll treat ourselves to a wonderful cup of coffee or cappuccino at our favorite little nook and enjoy the civility of it all."

❧

Create a "wall of friends" in your home, with pictures of as many of your friends as you can find, in frames to match their personalities.

❧

Organize a female film fest for an evening or Sunday afternoon at your home. We recommend *Strangers in Good Company*, *Fried Green Tomatoes*, *Julia*, *Postcards from the Edge*, *Thelma and Louise*, *The Color Purple*, *The Women*, *Boys on the Side*, and *Hannah and Her Sisters*. These are great movies about the strengths and weaknesses of women and the intricacies of their relationships, and they are sure to spawn a lot of discussion.

Just Between Us

Sometimes we rely on our girlfriends to help us grow. We might need to become more assertive, more honest about our feelings, or more confident in our decisions. Here are a few girlfriend rituals that women have used to strengthen, not only their relationship, but also their own personal growth.

Assert yourself! Claudette and her friend found themselves often apologizing to each other, as well as to others in their lives, even when circumstances didn't warrant it. To remedy the habit, for six weeks she and her friend each put a quarter in a jar every time either one of them said "sorry." They shared a dinner celebrating their newly found self-esteem by using the accumulated money to pay for the meal.

Celebrate a friend's new beginning (or an ending) with a spiritual housecleaning. Helen told us about a ritual her group of friends enjoys whenever one of them moves into a new home or ends a relationship. "First, we meet at the house, in a serious mood initially, and burn sage. Then we go through the rooms of the house with lit candles. Drawing from a Jewish tradition, we bring salt to sprinkle through the house to purify it. It starts out seriously — sometimes there are tears as an ending is mourned — but by the end of it we're a raucous group, opening the closets and throwing salt in. It's so much fun!"

Include your friends in your recovery. Nina, who was facing the truth of her own child abuse, composed a ritual to acknowledge that the image of her father that she held as a child had died and had been replaced by the truth. "I asked two of my friends to come and witness me burning items that symbolized my relationship with my father. As the items burned in the fireplace, I read the eulogy of the relationship between my father and me. One friend brought candles, and the other brought incense. It was a big step for me to ask them to support me and to let them give me what I had requested. It was very symbolic to me."

Enjoy being girls again. Get your friends together for a "big girl" slumber party. Or take them to the beach to build a huge sand castle. It's never too late to enjoy girlhood. Stop worrying what people will think!

Discussion Groups

Anne Morrow Lindbergh observed in the midseventies in her book *Gift from the Sea:*

> The best "growing ground" for women, however, may be in the widespread mushrooming of women's groups of all types and sizes. Women are talking to each other, not simply in private in the kitchen, in the nursery, or over the back fence, as they have done through the ages, but in public groups. They are airing their problems, discovering themselves, and comparing their experiences.[1]

Discussion groups come in many sizes and formats. All that is required is two or more women. Here are some of the ideas we've collected:

Start a breakfast club. We heard of a group of women living in a small town who go to the local café each Saturday morning to tell their stories and problems. They have created a sense of community and a place women can share their experiences, their goodwill, and their humor.

❧

Join a book club, or start one of your own by gathering other women who enjoy books, agreeing on a book to read, and then meeting again to discuss the book and how it relates to your own lives. Cathie told us she has belonged to the same book club since 1965.

❧

Say it with flowers. One group of women assembles for discussion every month, each woman bringing a flower that represents herself on that day. When all the women are assembled, a beautiful bouquet has been formed, and it changes from meeting to meeting.

❧

Host an international night. Claudette said her group of friends used to have dinners once a month organized around the theme of a particular country, and each guest would have to come dressed in garb associated with that country.

Get on the Internet. Molly uses her online service to connect with her girlfriends. They have developed a newsletter to publish poems and reviews and share ideas. There is a service which we heard about called "Women's Wire," an electronic community where women can log on and talk about their concerns and issues.

A Friendship Ritual

Sue Thoele, author of *The Woman's Book of Courage* and other titles, wanted to formalize her sisterhood with her best friend, Bonnie Hampton, a psychotherapist. As Sue relayed to us, "I really love ritual. I think it touches you at a deep level that is wordless." Bonnie, by her own admission, is "more intellectually than spiritually grounded" so was not sure that this ritual business was something she wanted to do. However, because she valued the friendship, she was willing to try it. They spontaneously developed their own ritual, which focused on their relationship and how their friendship supported them in their own lives.

These are the ingredients they used, but you should use whatever has meaning for you and your friend:

Pink, red, and white rose petals.

A statue of a figure that represents their friendship to them.

A list of attributes that each wishes to have the other friend safeguard in the future.

Both women are in their midfifties, and each looks to the other to be an important part of her life as they grow older. In their ritual, they sat knee to knee, forehead to forehead, and spoke of the items that they had collected. The rose petals stood for patience (pink), passion (red), and purity (white), and as they examined each, they talked of the significance of that emotion or quality in their present and future lives. As Sue said, "We are going to get old, and we have always said that we promise to get old together. In our ritual, we had very specific requests of each other, and we promised what we would be and do for each other as we age."

Each took something away from the ritual that went beyond words—feelings that only a ceremony can solidify. Sue remembers, "It was wonderful. I am a very security-conscious person. This formalized bond may not change my actions at all, but it adds a different dimension to my life."

Bonnie, on the other hand, noted, "I think of myself as a risk taker. Having that ritual allows me to continue to take risks because I know that Sue will take care of me and that she will help my family take care of me in a way that I want. That safe base allows me to take even more risk."

Plan your own ritual with your friend. How you do it and what you use to signify your relationship are not important. Merely taking the time, indicating to each other what you value about each other, or entrusting each other with your ultimate goals or worries are significant. These actions indicate that you recognize the centrality of this relationship to your lives.

Endnotes

TELLING OUR STORIES

1. Janet L. Surrey, Ph.D., "The 'Self-in-Relation': A Theory of Women's Development", *Work in Progress* n13, 1985, 2.

2. Quoted in Janet L. Surrey, Ph.D., "The 'Self-in-Relation': A Theory of Women's Development", *Work in Progress* n13, 1985, 1.

3. Sheila Ruth, *Issues in Feminism: An Introduction to Women's Studies* (Mountain View, CA: Mayfield Publishing Company, 1990), 450–51.

4. Ibid.

5. Ibid., 88.

6. Ibid., 150.

7. Quoted in Autumn Stephens, *Wild Words from Wild Women* (Berkeley: Conari Press, 1993), 49.

8. Sheila Ruth, *Issues in Feminism: An Introduction to Women's Studies* (Mountain View, CA: Mayfield Publishing Company, 1990), 81.

9. Susan J. Douglas, *Where the Girls Are: Growing Up Female with the Mass Media* (New York: Times Books, 1994), 14.

10. Ibid., 9.

11. Quoted in Autumn Stephens, *Wild Words from Wild Women* (Berkeley: Conari Press, 1993), 165.

12. Deborah Tannen, *You Just Don't Understand: Women and Men in Conversation* (New York: Ballantine, 1991), 52–53.

13. Sheila Ruth, *Issues in Feminism: An Introduction to Women's Studies* (Mountain View, CA: Mayfield Publishing Company, 1990), 400.

14. Quoted in Rosalie Maggio, *The Beacon Book of Quotations by Women* (Boston: Beacon Press, 1992), 140.

15. Quoted in Autumn Stephens, *Wild Words from Wild Women* (Berkeley: Conari Press, 1993), 7.

16. Quoted in Rosalie Maggio, *The Beacon Book of Quotations by Women* (Boston: Beacon Press, 1992), 243.

FACES OF FRIENDSHIP

1. Lillian B. Rubin, *Just Friends: The Role of Friendship in Our Lives* (New York: HarperCollins, 1985), 43.

2. Ibid.

3. Ibid.

4. Rosemarie Lennon, "Childhood Friends Shape Our Lives Forever," *For Women First,* July 3, 1995, 83.

5. Quoted in Rosemarie Lennon, "Childhood Friends Shape Our Lives Forever," *For Women First,* July 3, 1995, 83.

6. Ibid., 87.

7. Quoted in *The Quotable Woman* (Philadelphia: Running Press, 1991), 113.

8. Fay Weldon, *Praxis* (New York: Penguin, 1990), 147.

9. Quoted in *The Quotable Woman* (Philadelphia: Running Press, 1991), 122.

10. Excerpted from radio interview with Olive Dickason and Carlotta Blue, hosted by Peter Gzowski, Canadian Broadcasting Corp., "Morningside."

11. *Webster's New Collegiate Dictionary* (Springfield, MA: G. & C. Merriam Company, 1975), 373.

12. Anna Quindlen, "Heroine Addiction" in *Thinking Out Loud: On the Personal, the Political, the Public, and the Private* (New York: Ballantine/Fawcett, 1993), 267.

13. Patricia Hampl, "The Whole Anne Frank," *The New York Times Book Review, The New York Times,* March 5, 1995, 1, 21.

14. Lillian B. Rubin, *Just Friends: The Role of Friendship in Our Lives* (New York: HarperCollins, 1985), 28.

15. Ibid., 31.

16. Sherry Ruth Anderson and Patricia Hopkins, *The Feminine Face of God: The Unfolding of the Sacred in Women* (New York: Bantam, 1991), 212.

17. Quoted in *The Quotable Woman* (Philadelphia: Running Press, 1991), 160.

18. Quoted in Julia Gilden and Mark Friedman, *Woman to Woman: Entertaining and Enlightening Quotes by Women About Women* (New York: Dell, 1994), 39.

19. Quoted in *The Quotable Woman* (Philadelphia: Running Press, 1991), 44.

20. Quoted in Elaine Partnow, ed., *The New Quotable Woman: The Definitive Treasury of Notable Words by Women from Eve to the Present* (New York: Penguin, 1993), 650.

21. Stephanie Salter, "Lake Ladies: Grown-up Kids at 40," *San Francisco Examiner*, April 25, 1989, A-21.

WOMEN'S RITES

1. Anne Morrow Lindbergh, *Gift from the Sea* (New York: Random House, 1975), 137.

Recommended Reading

FICTION:

Atwood, Margaret. *The Robber Bride*. (New York: Doubleday) 1993.

Austen, Jane. *Pride and Prejudice*. (New York: Dell) 1978.

Bowles, Jane. *Two Serious Ladies*. (New York: E.P. Dutton, Inc.) 1984.

Fisher, Carrie. *Postcards From the Edge*. (New York: Pocket Books) 1987.

Flagg, Fannie. *Fried Green Tomatoes at the Whistle Stop Cafe*. (New York: McGraw-Hill Book Company) 1988.

Hailey, Elizabeth Forsythe. *A Woman of Independent Means*. (New York: Dell) 1991.

McMillan, Terry. *Waiting to Exhale*. (New York: Pocket Books) 1994.

Morrison, Toni. *Sula*. (New York: Penguin) 1982.

Naylor, Gloria. *The Women of Brewster Place*. (New York: Viking) 1982.

Tan, Amy. *The Joy Luck Club*. (New York: Ballantine) 1992.

Walker, Alice. *The Color Purple*. (New York: Pocket Books) 1983.

Weldon, Fay. *Praxis*. (New York: Penguin) 1990.

NONFICTION:

Anderson, Sherry Ruth, and Patricia Hopkins. *Feminine Face of God: The Unfolding of the Sacred in Women*. (New York: Bantam) 1992.

Bender, Sue. *Plain and Simple: A Woman's Journey to the Amish*. (San Francisco: HarperCollins) 1991.

Bernstein, Arlene. *Growing Season*. (Berkeley, CA: Wildcat Canyon Press) 1995.

De Beauvoir, Simone. *The Second Sex*. (New York: Random House) 1989.

Douglas, Susan J. *Where the Girls Are: Growing Up Female with the Mass Media*. (New York: Times Books) 1994.

Estés, Clarissa Pinkola, Ph.D. *Women Who Run With the Wolves: Myths and Stories of the Wild Woman Archetype*. (New York: Ballantine) 1992.

Friedan, Betty. *The Feminine Mystique*. (New York: Dell) 1984.

Gilligan, Carol. *In a Different Voice: Psychological Theory and Women's Development.* (Cambridge, MA: Harvard University Press) 1993.

Gilligan, Carol, Nona P. Lyons, and Trudy J. Hanmer. *Making Connections: The Relational Worlds of Adolescent Girls at Emma Willard School.* (Cambridge, MA: Harvard University Press) 1990.

Hart, Judy. *Love, Judy: Letters of Hope and Healing for Women With Breast Cancer.* (Berkeley, CA: Conari Press) 1993.

Hellman, Lillian. *Pentimento.* (Boston: Little, Brown and Company) 1973.

Kenyon, Olga, ed. *800 Years of Women's Letters.* (New York: Penguin) 1992.

Kidd, Sue Monk. *Circle of Trees.* (San Francisco: HarperCollins) In press, 1996.

Lindbergh, Anne Morrow. *Gift from the Sea.* (New York: Random House) 1975.

Louden, Jennifer. *The Woman's Comfort Book: A Self-Nurturing Guide for Restoring Balance in Your Life.* (San Francisco: HarperCollins) 1992.

Martz, Sandra Haldeman, ed. *When I Am An Old Woman I Shall Wear Purple* (Watsonville, CA: Papier-Mache Press) 1987.

Quindlen, Anna. *Thinking Out Loud: On the Personal, the Political, the Public, and the Private.* (New York: Ballantine/Fawcett) 1993.

Rubin, Lillian B. *Just Friends: The Role of Friendship in Our Lives.* (New York: HarperCollins) 1985.

Schaef, Anne Wilson. *Women's Reality: An Emerging Female System in a White Male Society.* (San Francisco: HarperCollins) 1992.

Shanley, Mary Kay. *She Taught Me to Eat Artichokes: The Discovery of the Heart of Friendship.* Illustrations by Paul Micich. (Marshalltown, IA: Sta-Kris, Inc.) 1993.

Tannen, Deborah. *You Just Don't Understand: Women and Men in Conversation* (New York: Ballantine) 1991.

Thoele, Sue Patton. *The Woman's Book of Courage: Meditations for Empowerment and Peace of Mind* (Berkeley, CA: Conari Press) 1991.

Woolf, Virginia. *A Room of One's Own.* (San Diego: Harcourt Brace Jovanovich) 1957.

About the Authors

CARMEN RENEE BERRY is a well-known speaker and author. As a former psychotherapist, and now a certified body worker, she has dedicated herself to the integration of the body, the emotions, the spirit, and the mind in promoting healthy lifestyles for people of all ages.

Girlfriends is Carmen's seventh book. Her other publications are *Your Body Never Lies* (PageMill Press), *Who's to Blame?* (Piñon Press), co-authored with Mark Baker, Ph.D., *When Helping You Is Hurting Me* (HarperCollins), *Are You Having Fun Yet?* (Thomas Nelson), *How to Escape the Messiah Trap: A Workbook* (Harper Collins), and *Loving Yourself As Your Neighbor* (HarperCollins), co-authored with Mark Taylor, Ph.D.

Carmen has an M.S.W. from the University of Southern California and a master's degree in Social Sciences from the University of Northern Arizona. When not on the road, her home is in Pasadena, California, where she enjoys her supportive network of friends.

TAMARA TRAEDER is the Publisher of PageMill Press, a publisher of psychology titles for the mental health professional and their clients. Before entering the publishing field, she practiced corporate law for seven years in San Francisco, and continues to practice law in the area of intellectual property.

Tamara graduated from the University of Virginia Law School in 1985 and graduated from the University of Missouri with a liberal arts degree in 1982.

Tamara lives in Berkeley, California, and thinks that her friends are among her greatest blessings. This is her first book.

Tell Us About Your Girlfriend

Do you have an extraordinary story of friendship you would like to share? Send your story to the address below and be sure to include your name, address and phone number. We will contact you if we decide it is appropriate for any new editions of the book.

Wildcat Canyon Press publishes books with a focus on spirituality, personal growth, women's issues, home and family. Whether books of meditations, short essays or how-to texts, they are designed to enlighten the hearts and souls of readers. For a catalog of our publications please write:

Wildcat Canyon Press
2716 Ninth Street
Berkeley, California 94710
Phone 510-848-3600
Fax 510-848-1326

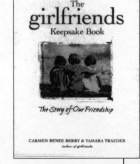